FIELD DRESSING AND BUTCHERING DEER

Books by Monte Burch

Field Dressing and Butchering Upland Birds, Waterfowl, and Wild Turkeys
Field Dressing and Butchering Rabbits, Squirrels, and Other Small Game
Field Dressing and Butchering Big Game
The Field & Stream All-Terrain-Vehicle Handbook
Denny Brauer's Jig Fishing Secrets
Denny Brauer's Winning Tournament Tactics
Black Bass Basics
Guide to Calling & Rattling Whitetail Bucks
Guide to Successful Turkey Calling
Guide to Calling & Decoying Waterfowl
Guide to Successful Predator Calling
Pocket Guide to Seasonal Largemouth Bass Patterns
Pocket Guide to Seasonal Walleye Tactics
Pocket Guide to Old Time Catfish Techniques
Pocket Guide to Field Dressing, Butchering & Cooking Deer
Pocket Guide to Bowhunting Whitetail Deer
Pocket Guide to Spring & Fall Turkey Hunting
Guide to Fishing, Hunting & Camping Truman
The Pro's Guide to Fishing Missouri Lakes
Waterfowling, A Sportsman's Handbook
Modern Waterfowl Hunting
Shotgunner's Guide
Gun Care and Repair
Outdoorsman's Fix-It Book
Outdoorsman's Workshop
Building and Equipping the Garden and Small Farm Workshop
Basic House Wiring
Complete Guide to Building Log Homes
Children's Toys and Furniture
64 Yard and Garden Projects You Can Build
How to Build 50 Classic Furniture Reproductions
Tile Indoors and Out
The Home Cabinetmaker
How to Build Small Barns & Outbuildings
Masonry & Concrete
Pole Building Projects
Building Small Barns, Sheds & Shelters
Home Canning & Preserving (w/Joan Burch)
Building Mediterranean Furniture (w/Jay Hedden)
Fireplaces (w/Robert Jones)
The Homeowner's Complete Manual of Repair and Improvement (w/3 others)
The Good Earth Almanac Series
Survival Handbook
Old-Time Recipes
Natural Gardening Handbook

FIELD DRESSING AND BUTCHERING DEER

Step-by-Step Instructions, from Field to Table

Monte Burch

The Lyons Press
Guilford, Connecticut
An imprint of The Globe Pequot Press

The Lyons Press is an imprint of The Globe Pequot Press.

Printed in the United States of America

Designed by Compset, Inc.

10 9 8 7 6 5 4 3 2 1

Library of Congress Cataloging-in-Publication Data is available on file.

Contents

Introduction

The first glimmering rays of dawn are just breaking the timbered skyline to the east when you spot movement in the brush near the edge of the old logging road. It's the third morning in a row you've sat in the stand strapped 20 feet up the trunk of a white oak, and you remember the doe and two young that visit about this time each morning. They appear almost magically to sniff and mill around the bare spot of ground located about 50 yards away at the edge of the old road. They were indeed welcome company, as were the two button bucks that cautiously sniffed your mock scrape then scrambled away into the timber almost immediately.

Movement again. You unconsciously stiffen, heart pounding as you wait for a better glimpse. Then he steps into the opening, the hackle hair on his back ruffled. He approaches the scrape in short, stiff-legged steps, almost stomping, all the while making short, sharp grunts. Even without the magnificent rack on his head and the huge swelled neck, it's no doubt this is the king of the woods. As he turns to sniff the overhanging branch over the scrape, you slowly raise your rifle, place the crosshairs just behind his shoulder, take a deep breath and, just as you begin to let the breath out, carefully and slowly squeeze the trigger.

Before we left the house that cold November morning, my son Mark, then 12, and I went over our signals again. We were hunting about a quarter mile apart and had arranged a set of signals for him to let me know his hunting situation. If he quit and went back to the house before I came in, he was supposed to honk the car horn once. If he collected a deer, it was down, and everything was OK, he was to honk twice. I could then hunt more or eventually work my way to his stand. If he knocked a deer down and it escaped or

More than eleven million hunters hit the woods each fall in hopes of collecting a whitetail deer.

he had other problems, he was supposed to honk the car horn three times.

Thirty minutes into the morning hunt, I was busy enjoying the antics of a couple of yearling bucks mock fighting in front of my stand when I heard his 30–30 go off. Within seconds, a war whoop

For some, a trophy buck is their goal.

echoed over the Ozark hilltops. I laughed out loud. Forget worrying about the signals. I knew he had a deer on the ground—his first. I started walking back to the house to get the tractor but hadn't gotten a hundred yards when I heard the car horn honk twice. He had covered the quarter mile distance in less time than a star track runner and was announcing his success with glee. As I walked up the hillside to the farmyard he ran grinning toward me.

"I got one, I got one," he excitedly exclaimed. "And boy, is it a big one."

For others, meat for the table is the main reason for the hunt.

Several minutes later we stood over his downed deer, and indeed it was a big animal—a big old doe. We hugged, laughed, and danced around the animal while all the time he excitedly told and retold the story of his hunt. As I started to field dress the doe I thought, "What a trophy. He'll remember this the rest of his life. I know I will."

Regardless of whether going after a wall hanger or meat for the table, more than 11 million hunters hit the woods each fall in search of America's undisputed favorite big game animal: whitetail deer. Although not every hunter will find a deer in his sights, many freezers are stocked with venison steaks, roasts, and burger each deer season. Some say taking a deer is the highlight of every hunt, but many feel that the best part of deer hunting comes later at the dinner table.

"People hunt for a lot of reasons, but every hunter agrees that eating game is an essential part of the hunting experience," says J. D. Peer, hunter education coordinator for the Oklahoma Department of Wildlife Conservation. "It's the key ingredient that connects the hunter to the game, that makes us participants in the cycle of life in the natural world instead of just being observers. Partaking of game gives a hunter a deeper respect and reverence for that animal than those who don't understand the connection."

Maria Beierschmitt, a food science specialist masters graduate from the University of Missouri-Columbia, would like to see more people eat venison. She would actually like to see venison, already considered a healthy red meat, next to beef, pork, and chicken in the grocer's meat case.

"In Europe, venison is considered gourmet food fit for royalty, but in the United States, it is considered roadkill," Beierschmitt said. "Knowing more about the meat allows us to build consumer acceptance."

Using samples of Missouri white-tailed deer, Beierschmitt looked at six properties of venison: acidity, fat content, moisture content, its ability to retain moisture when heated and when put under pressure, and its water activity to determine the microbial survival rate and shelf life. Many results were similar to beef, but fat content results revealed why venison is an attractive alternative.

"If beef is what's for dinner and pork the other white meat, then venison is the healthy red meat," she said. "Wild game tends to be very lean. Our samples contained around 2 percent fat as opposed to the 30 percent fat content found in some ground beef."

Venison has been a staple at our household for more than three decades. Our kids and now grandkids grew up eating venison. We've prepared and cooked it just about every manner possible— and it's still a favorite not only with our family but with our guests as well. Many of our guests have never eaten venison before and are often quite surprised at the quality of the meat being served.

Over the years I've also taught numerous neighbors, beginning hunters, youngsters, and others the skills of field dressing and butchering. It's not hard to do. It is a basic life skill that provides a feeling of independence, and you control the quality of meat as well as types of cuts you prefer.

To get the most enjoyment from your harvest, however, you need to take proper care of the meat from the beginning of the shot until you place it on the table. If properly handled, you'll be able to enjoy many meals of lean, high-protein meat that is 100 percent natural, with no additives or preservatives. Although the majority of the deer harvested are whitetails, the same techniques of field dressing, butchering, and cooking work as well for mule deer and blacktails. In this book we go from basic field dressing through skinning, butchering, and proper cooking methods. I even provide a number of venison recipes my family, friends, and some of my hunting buddies have enjoyed.

Here's to good luck with your hunts and great venison on the table.

Preface

U nfortunately, I hear a lot of hunters comment that they like to deer hunt, but their family doesn't like deer meat. Venison can be exquisite or indeed absolutely terrible to eat for a number of reasons.

The first step to quality meat begins in the field. You wouldn't purposely pick an old, tough bull for steaks to grill. The finest beef comes from younger animals, and venison is the same. Even old does can be tough, although they tend to be less gamey flavored than an old, monarch buck in full rut. If possible, pick a young, healthy animal if your main purpose is table fare.

Studies have shown that a stressed animal produces lower quality meat. An animal that has been improperly shot and runs a great distance is a prime example. By the same token, where the animal is shot is also important. An animal that is hit cleanly in a vital area and dies instantly will produce better tasting meat than one that is gut shot and runs a long distance. For that reason, regardless of whether hunting with a bow or gun, the first step is to learn proficiency with your equipment. Make sure your rifle is sighted in properly, and practice at a number of different yardages so you can confidently make a clean killing shot. If a bowhunter, spend time year-round practicing with your bow at a number of different yardages and from practice tree-stand locations so you learn how to shoot from different angles and distances.

Make as clean and as quick a kill as possible. Our family has butchered their own meat for generations, and I still do three to four hogs a year, a steer, and sometimes a half dozen or more deer, including some for friends and neighbors. An animal that runs a long distance after the shot is adrenalin charged, which has an effect on the meat flavor. Blood and lactic acid is pumped through the veins. "The meat will be fiery," my granddad used to say about a hog that hadn't been killed cleanly during the community butchering. And I've found over the years that he was absolutely right. For

Venison can provide great tasting table fare—or be inedible, depending on several factors. The first is to make a clean, quick kill.

that reason, hogs were killed with a single .22 pellet into the brain while standing quietly in their pen. Done correctly, the animal drops in its tracks. Several years ago I got a firsthand example of poor-quality meat that was a result of stress. I was helping a neighbor butcher a pig, and his shot was not correctly placed. Shot in the head but not dead, the terrified pig busted out of his pen and headed for the back forty. We finally caught up to the squealing animal in the truck and were able to make a finishing shot. After butchering, the meat had flecks of blood throughout, and the hams didn't cure properly.

Placement of your shot and when it is made is very important. If you want the best in venison, don't shoot at a running animal. The best shot is when the animal is unalarmed and standing still. Pick your shot and wait, if possible, for the best moment. Traditional shot locations are the heart and lung area, often called the "boiler room" by many old-time deer hunters. Neck shots are, however, the best, if they are presented, as there is less waste damage and waste of meat. The worst is a gut-shot animal. I've dressed a few and hate it. Bits and pieces of intestine contents are sprayed

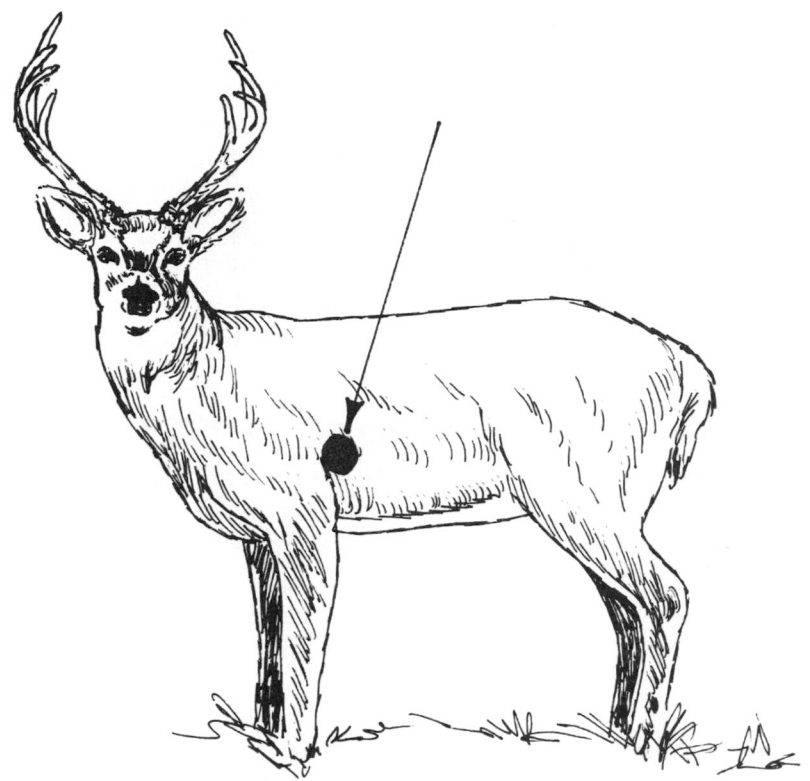

Shot placement is extremely important. The most common shot is just behind the shoulder to hit the lungs.

throughout much of the center of the body and even driven into the surrounding muscles.

Regardless of whether you wish to butcher and prepare the meat yourself or have it done by professionals, the correct steps made in the field can greatly affect the palatability of your venison.

Studies done by Joyce A. Hosch and Milo Shult for Texas A & M reveal a great deal of information on the subject. The objectives of the study were to determine the effects of stress at the time of death, type of field dress, aging, time of skinning, and sex on the quality of deer meat. Other objectives were to determine the numbers and types of bacteria found on the surface of deer carcasses and to develop methods for the production of smoked deer-meat products, such as sausages and hams. Thirty-six animals were harvested from two ranches located about 20 miles north of Hondo, Texas. Five factors involved in slaughtering and handling deer were chosen to determine their effects on the quality of venison: sex, delayed skinning, stress, delayed field dress, and cold-storage aging. Five test groups with treatment and a control group were included. Taste-panel evaluations were made of the meat from the six groups. The five taste classifications included flavor intensity, flavor desirability, juiciness, tenderness, and overall satisfaction. The taste panel decided that the sex of the animal determined the intensity (gamey) flavor of the deer meat. Male animals rated higher in flavor intensity. An increase in flavor intensity was also found in female animals aged for 1 week in a cooler. This intensity, however, was not the same (gamey) flavor associated with the male animal. The panel decided aging definitely produced a more desirable flavor. Venison is basically a dry meat, and one factor discovered is that the dryness was increased by hanging the carcass with the skin off. Tenderness is a most important quality of any meat. It was discovered there is a significant difference in tenderness between animals that were stressed or excited (gut shot) and those that were not.

The age and sex of the animal can also be a major factor in taste and tenderness. Male animals, especially older bucks, have a more intense "gamey" flavor.

Stressed animals entered rigor mortis (death stiffening) earlier, causing a noticeable decrease in tenderness. Aging the carcass, however, created more tenderness. The aging process not only retards and extends rigor but tends to increase the water-holding capacity of the meat, both of which are helpful in the tenderizing process.

Taste testers discovered overall satisfaction to be a combination of the desired traits. During the test demonstration, the group of animals showing the highest overall satisfaction were female animals aged 1 week. They discovered that boning the hams before aging decreased tenderness. This is because the bone serves as muscle attachment. When the bone is removed, the muscles, which are in an unnatural state, are allowed to contract more because there is no attachment. This reduces tenderness.

As the Texas studies have also shown, there is a good deal of difference in taste and palatability between does and bucks. Many hunters don't have the choice of whether to take a buck or doe; a buck may be all that is allowed, or it may simply be a matter of taking the first deer that comes by. But if you do have a choice, then you need to decide if you prefer to pick out the best meat animal or wait for a big set of horns. The two are not necessarily compatible. The single best choice is a young animal: Young does or spike bucks simply can't be beat. The next choice would be an older doe; because she would be larger in body size, she would provide more meat. The last choice would be a mature buck, particularly during the rut. Meat from older bucks can also be quite palatable if properly aged and prepared.

There is also a great deal of difference in the taste of deer according to the forage foods available. Deer that are fattened on corn or are primarily feeding on white oak acorns will be much more palatable than deer that must forage on foods such as buckbrush. By the same token, there is simply a variety of taste in individual animals. A buck taken right at the first of the rut will taste different than one taken at the last of the rut. A doe that is nursing young will have a stronger flavor than one that isn't.

CHAPTER 1

Tools and Equipment

Having the proper tools and equipment for field dressing and butchering deer is extremely important. A good, clean work space for butchering is essential. The number of tools and amount of equipment and work space needed depends on the amount of field dressing and butchering you intend to do. If you only kill one deer a year, you'll probably need fewer tools than someone in a deer-hunting family or deer-hunting camp who is involved in butchering several animals.

CUTTING AND SHARPENING TOOLS

Field-dressing tools for deer begin with a good-quality field knife. This can be either a belt knife or large pocketknife. Many hunters make the mistake of purchasing too large a knife for the chore. On the other hand, it's hard to field dress with a puny pocketknife. The best knives for field dressing are not necessarily the best for all the skinning, caping, and butchering chores. A number of knives are designed specifically for the chores of field dressing. Most of these feature fairly short blades. Some have serrated backs for cutting through bones and a gut hook for easy gutting.

It's also best if the field dressing and skinning knife is kept separate and used for only those purposes. Other hunting-type knives can be used for heavier-duty purposes such as cutting ropes or wood pieces for firewood. I've owned and used a number of knives excellent for the chore. One is a Buck I've had for years. It features a 4¼ inch blade with a gut hook. One of the best knives on the market is the Katz Hunters Tool Knife that is four tools in one. It features a bone saw on the back of the blade along with a gut hook.

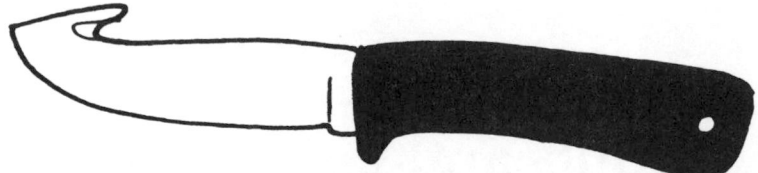

Field dressing knives should have fairly short blades. Those with gut hooks make the latter chore easier.

The 5½-inch blade is excellent XT80 stainless steel, available either plain or 50/50 plain and serrated. A checkered Kraton handle and leather lanyard ensure that you don't lose the knife during the chores.

Splitting the pelvic bone and the breast bone on deer and big game is important in order to properly remove all internal organs and allow blood to be removed from the cavity. On smaller deer, I've used a belt knife for the chore, and in some cases, I've used a belt knife with a rock or wooden log to split the pelvic bone. The

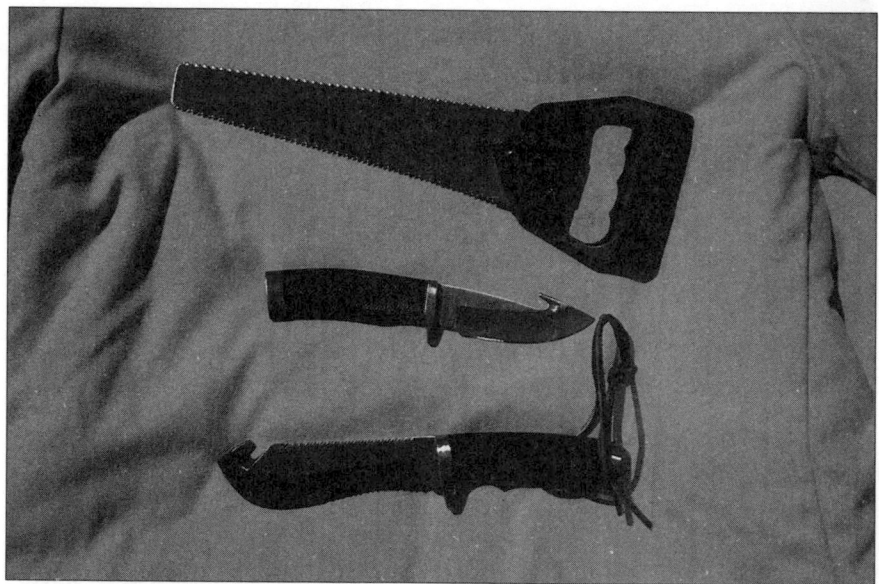

A game saw can be used for cutting the pelvic bone. Knives with a serrated saw blade, such as the Katz 3-in-1 Hunters Tool can also make short work of cutting the pelvic bone in field dressing.

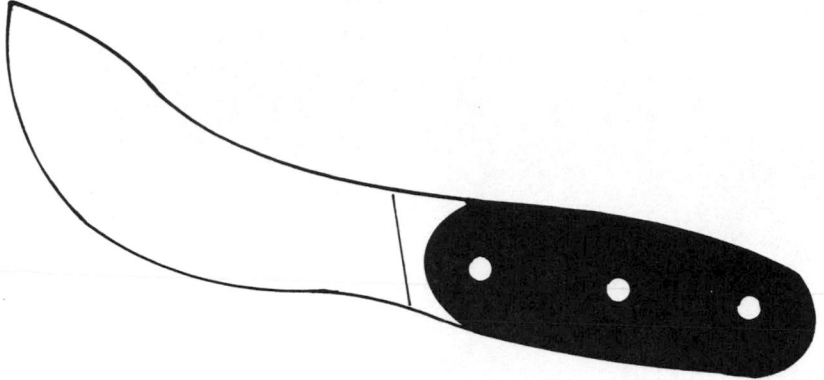

Skinning knives should also have relatively short blades with rounded curves to aid in "slicing" away skin. A number of these knives are also available, and some "field" belt knives have the proper shape.

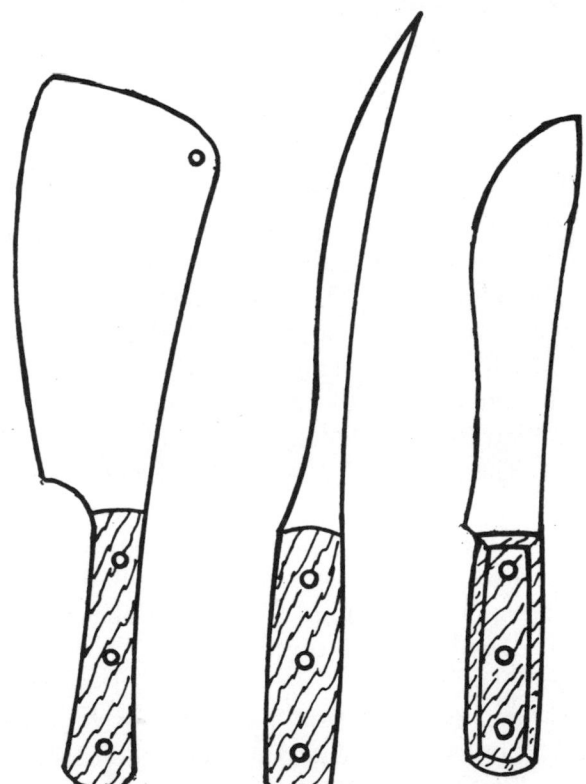

An assortment of butchering knives are also required.

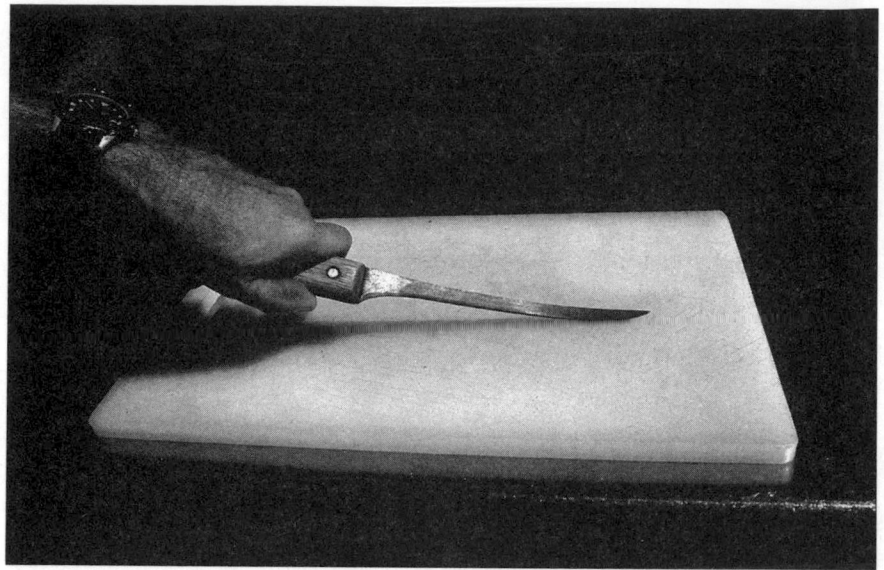

One knife should be a boning knife with a thin, flexible blade.

task is much easier, however, with the proper tools. A camp hatchet can be used for the chore and is also what I use when field dressing at camp or home. The Normark Hunters Skinning Axe is patterned after the centuries-old Eskimo Ulu knife and is great for all skinning chores. A lightweight, folding, and packable woodsman saw, however, is the best choice for in-the-field use. The Wyoming saw is especially designed for field dressing of big game and comes with carrying case. The multipurpose sportsman saws from Uncle Mike's feature a large T-handle that makes splitting pelvic and rib bones quick and easy. The Katz Hunters Tool has a very sturdy saw blade built into the back of the blade.

You may even need more than one knife in camp. The types of knives needed also depends on the chores. If the meat is to be deboned on the spot or in camp, a boning knife makes the chore much easier. If caping is to be done in camp, a short-bladed, relatively sharp point (drop-point) knife is also a good choice.

A wide variety of knives are required for butchering. These range from skinning knives, with their rounded points; long, thin pointed knives for boning out shoulders and roasts and trimming cuts; and long, heavy-bladed knives for slicing steaks and other cuts.

Boning knives are specialty knives. They should feature flexible blades that bend and slide around bones. They're more akin to fish fillet knives than any other styles. Unfortunately, I've not been able to locate good boning knives these days. I inherited one from my father and made my own from a Green River blade a number of years ago. The more knives you have on hand, the better off you are, as you don't have to stop to resharpen your knife every few minutes.

Knives are available in a variety of steels, ranging from stainless through several grades of carbon steel and combinations of steel. Stainless-steel knives are the hardest and soft carbon steel the softest. Stainless steel requires a great deal more effort to sharpen but holds the edge longer than the carbon metals. I prefer a stainless-steel knife for field dressing but use carbon-steel knives for butchering. I don't have to worry about the stainless-steel field-dressing knife quickly becoming dull while on a hunt. The carbon butcher knives, on the other hand, offer quicker touch-up with a handheld sharpening steel or hone during the butchering process.

Regardless of the type of knife and metal, it's important to have the knife extremely sharp when field dressing, skinning, butchering,

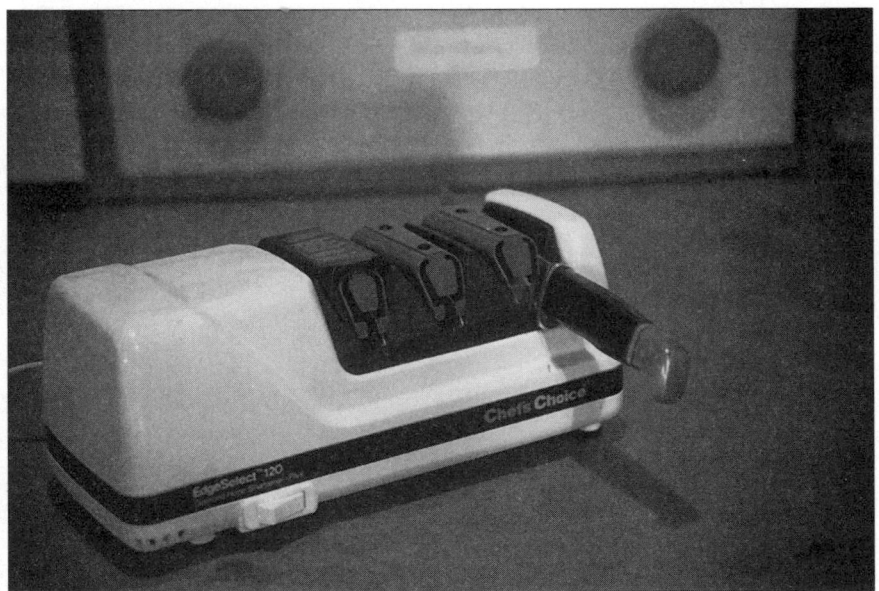

Sharpeners are also required to keep the knives sharp. Electric hones such as those from Chef'sChoice make the job easy.

or caping. In fact, when skinning and butchering, I keep a half-dozen knives sharpened and on hand so I don't have to stop and sharpen or hone a blade during the process.

A wide variety of sharpening devices is available, ranging from simple handheld stones to electric grinding wheels. My grandfather's old foot-turned grinding wheel did a great job of sharpening knives, and many of today's electric wheels also offer the same type of sharpening, only much easier. The Chef'sChoice Edge Select Professional #120 Diamond Hone Knife Sharpener from EdgeCraft Corporation is one of the best I've tested. It features patented precision guides for accurate control of the sharpening angle and foolproof results. The multistage design uses 100 percent diamond abrasives in stages 1 and 2, and a unique stropping and polishing stage 3, providing a triple-bevel razor edge quickly and easily. The company also has a number of manual sharpeners that can be kept by the worktable for quick and easy touch-up of knives.

FIELD-DRESSING KIT

In addition to a knife and hatchet or saw for splitting the pelvic bone and breastbone, a field-dressing kit containing several other items can make the chore easier and quicker for deer field dressing. All items can be carried in a recloseable plastic bag and will fit in a large pocket or a day or fanny pack. A second recloseable plastic bag can be used to transport the liver. A short piece of string should be included for tying off the anal opening. An 8-foot length of rope can be handy for dragging out the carcass, or in the case of pack-in, for hanging the game.

It's a good idea to wear disposable gloves for field-dressing chores. Not only does this help prevent the possibility of contracting Lyme Disease, but the gloves keep your hands clean, and cleanup is quick and easy. Simply peel the gloves off inside out, and place them in a separate plastic bag to be carried out and discarded once you're out of the woods. Hand-size gloves are fine, but veterinarian gloves that cover your lower arms will help keep your clothes cleaner. If you're in hunting camp, it's a good idea to have a nonscent clothes and body soap, such as Sport Wash from ATSKO, to clean up with. More than once I've field dressed a buddy's deer in the morning, then turned around and went right back to my stand to continue my hunt. I also carry a spray-on nonscent to spray my clothing and boots. If

A field dressing kit should contain disposable plastic gloves, a closeable plastic bag for liver, drag rope, and short piece of string. In hot dry weather, black pepper and mesh game bags may be needed to protect the meat.

you're packing in and the weather is hot and dry, you may also wish to carry a cheesecloth game bag, such as those from Alaska Game Bag Company, along with a can of pepper to protect the carcass from flies. The last item is a small sharpening stone. It's easy to dull a knife while field dressing, especially if you're doing more than one animal.

Skinning and Hanging Equipment

In some instances, deer are field-dressed, skinned, and hung in the field. In other instances, the hanging is done at camp or home. The amount of equipment needed depends on the number of game you commonly work up. Deer, especially more than one, require a meat pole. A large limb has sufficed for this chore for countless ages and will still work. In the absence of a sturdy limb in just the right place, a tripod of poles can be used to hoist big game in the field or in camp.

You can also build a game pole in camp by lashing a pole between two trees. If camp is a permanent affair and you don't have trees handy, or you do several deer a year at your home or camp,

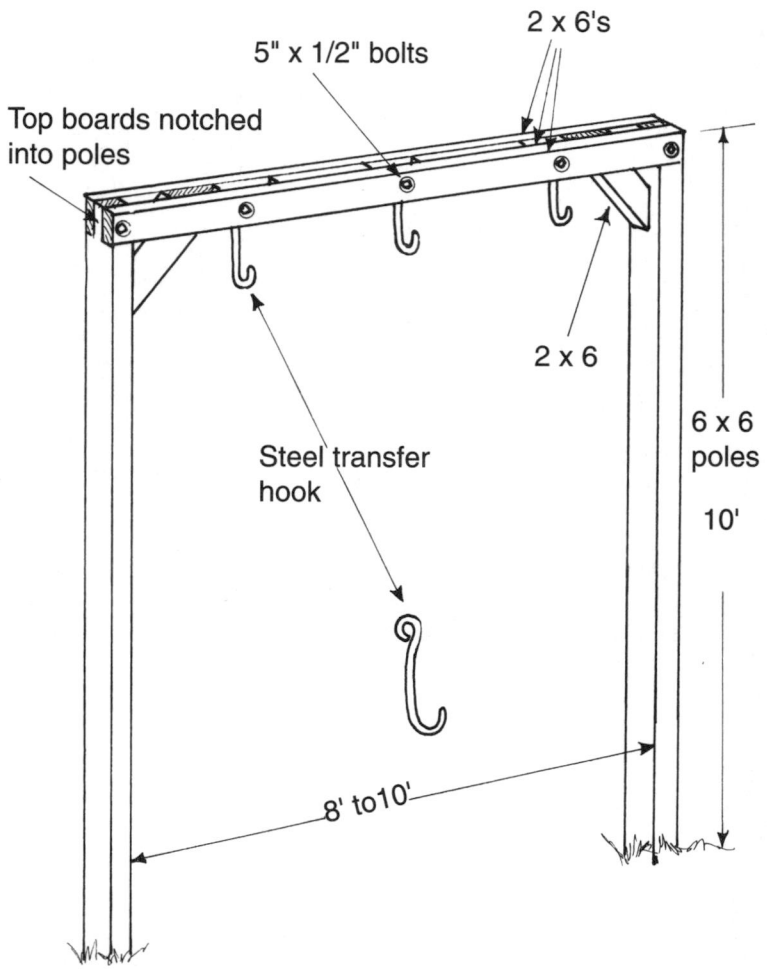

A game pole at camp, in your backyard, or even a barn or outbuilding can be a great help in hanging deer for skinning and quartering.

you may prefer a game pole. If at all possible, outside game poles should be located in the shade. A heavily reinforced beam in a barn or outbuilding is also a great hanging pole, especially if the building can be opened for ventilation to aid in cooling or closed down to protect the meat from dogs and other predators. I have a space in my barn specifically for the purpose, with a reinforced truss that can hang carcasses as large as a beef.

A game hoist or a block and tackle is also necessary for hoisting the larger animals safely in place. An ATV or vehicle winch can often be used for this purpose. These days, a number of companies also offer ATV game hoists that can be used to hoist deer-sized animals up for skinning. A transfer loop or meat hook is used to hold

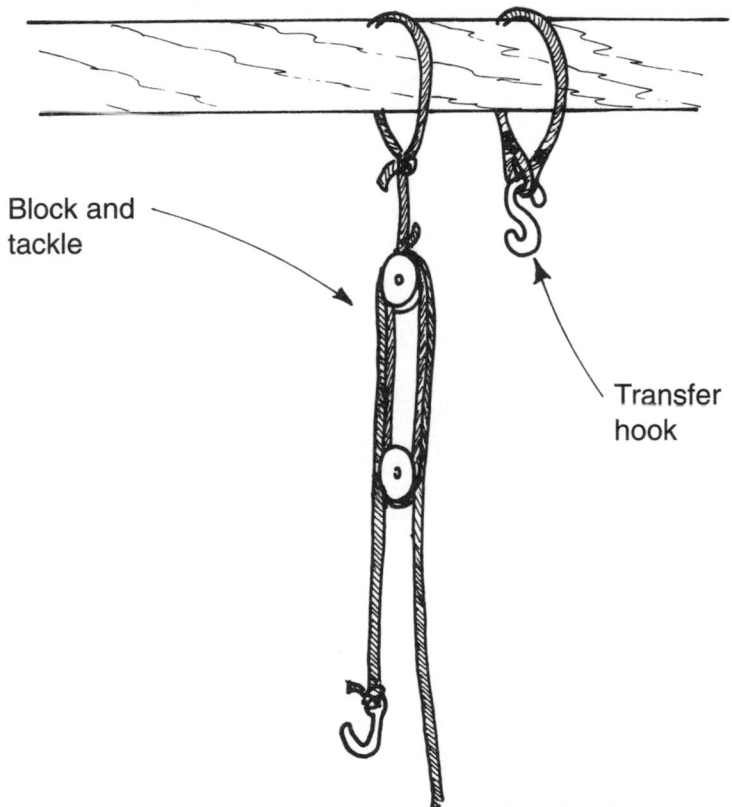

Block and tackle

Transfer hook

A game hoist, block and tackle, or electric winch can make short work of lifting the carcass up to the game pole.

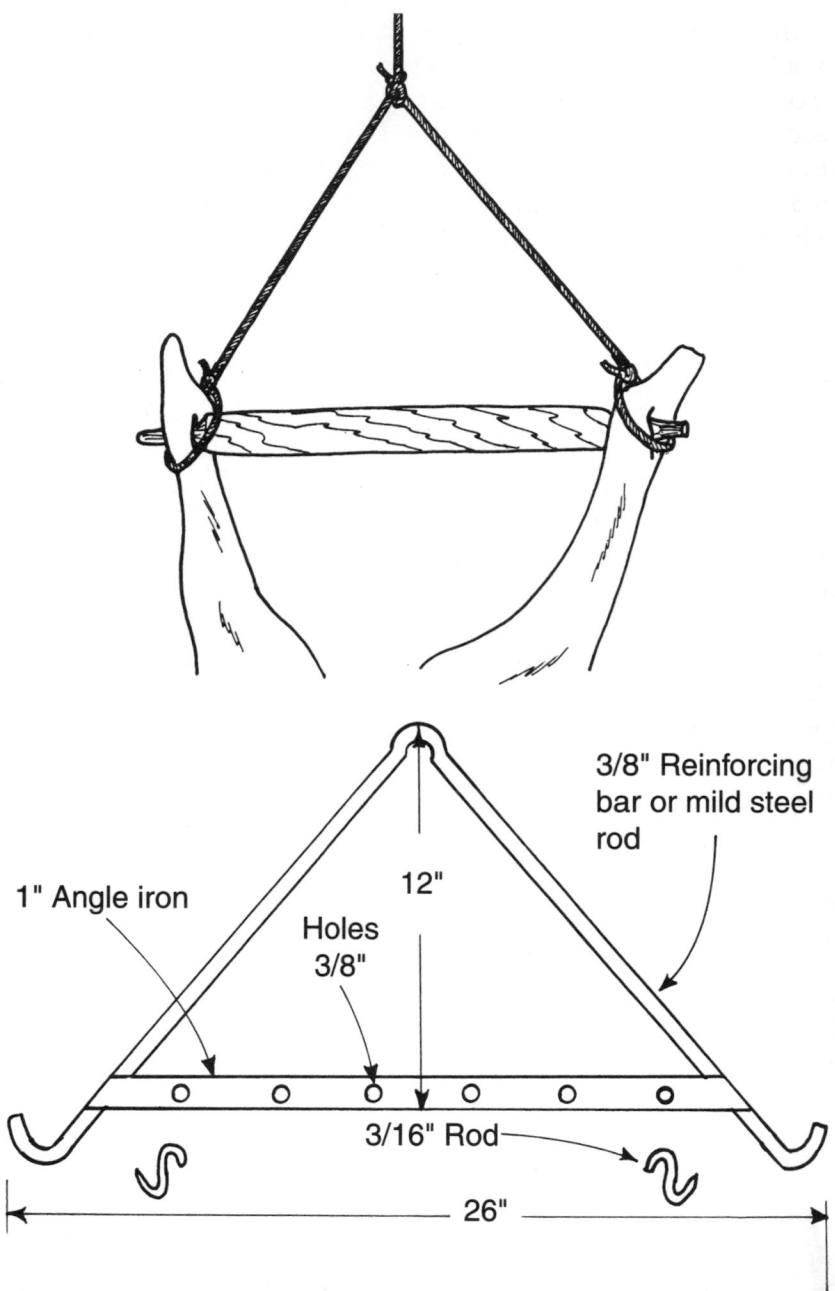

Gambrels are needed to spread the carcass for hanging, skinning, and quartering. In an emergency a stout stick can be used. You can purchase gambrels or make your own steel models as shown.

the carcass in place once it has been hoisted up. These hooks can also be used to hang quarters or halves.

For skinning and butchering, you'll also need gambrels or spreaders. These can be a simple stick with loops of string on the ends, commercial gambrels or spreaders, or you can make up your own as shown. A spreader stick to prop open the chest cavity can also be a great help.

BUTCHERING TOOLS

A hand meat saw is a necessity for the butchering. It's also a good idea to have several blades on hand. The meat saw is used to cut off the legs, split the carcass, and make rib and steak cuts and other cuts. The handheld meat saw also can be used for splitting the carcass if you prefer to butcher in that fashion, rather than boning or removing the loins. I also keep an electric chain saw on hand just for the task and don't use regular oil in it. Instead I use lightweight cooking oil to lubricate the chain and clean it thoroughly after use.

Other items you'll need include pans to hold meat as you butcher. Large plastic tubs can be used to hold meat cuts to be ground. Cutting surfaces are also important. Although wooden cutting boards are traditional, they're not as sanitary as some of the newer surfaces. Once wooden cutting boards become grooved from knives, it's hard to completely remove the blood and meat particles. The best surfaces for cutting are surfaces that don't become grooved with knife cuts yet can be cleaned and sanitized. It's a good idea to have one large surface, or at least a couple of smaller ones. My dad ran a cabinet shop for years and we recycled the plastic laminate sink cutouts as cutting boards. These work great, but they become grooved over time and need to be

A hand meat saw is needed for quartering and can also be used for making more traditional butcher cuts.

replaced. Lots of clean, soft rags are also important for wiping and cleaning your hands, cleaning surfaces, and removing hair from knife blades during the skinning process.

WORK SPACE

You can, of course, skin in your backyard and butcher on your kitchen table or countertop. Butchering, however, is messy, and a space set aside for the chore—outside or in a garage or outbuilding—is best. This doesn't have to be elaborate or involve a lot of space. And you can use the area for storage of other items when not needed for butchering.

You'll need a sturdy table with an easily cleanable top. This can be a plastic laminate top, or you can simply use oil cloth or plastic tablecloths for butchering if the top is wood. One of the best surfaces is stainless steel. It hoses down and cleans up quite easily and is sturdy and hard surfaced. You will still need a separate cut-

An easy-to-clean workspace, cutting boards, and tubs for holding meat are also required for butchering.

ting surface over it—stainless steel will scratch and quickly dulls knife blades. Several years ago, I bought two used stainless-steel school cafeteria kitchen tables at an auction, and they are one of the best investments I have ever made. I have one set up outside next to my garage with a work light over it and an outside plug nearby. I use it for everything from filleting fish to dressing wild turkeys and waterfowl to cutting up deer. I also have one set up in my garage for weather protection and those days when it's too hot or too cold to do outside butchering chores. Both of the tables were fairly low, and I added leg extenders to raise them to a comfortable, 36-inch working height. Low tables can cause back problems when standing and cutting up meat in a slightly bent-over position. Several years ago, I also made a table just for the purpose,

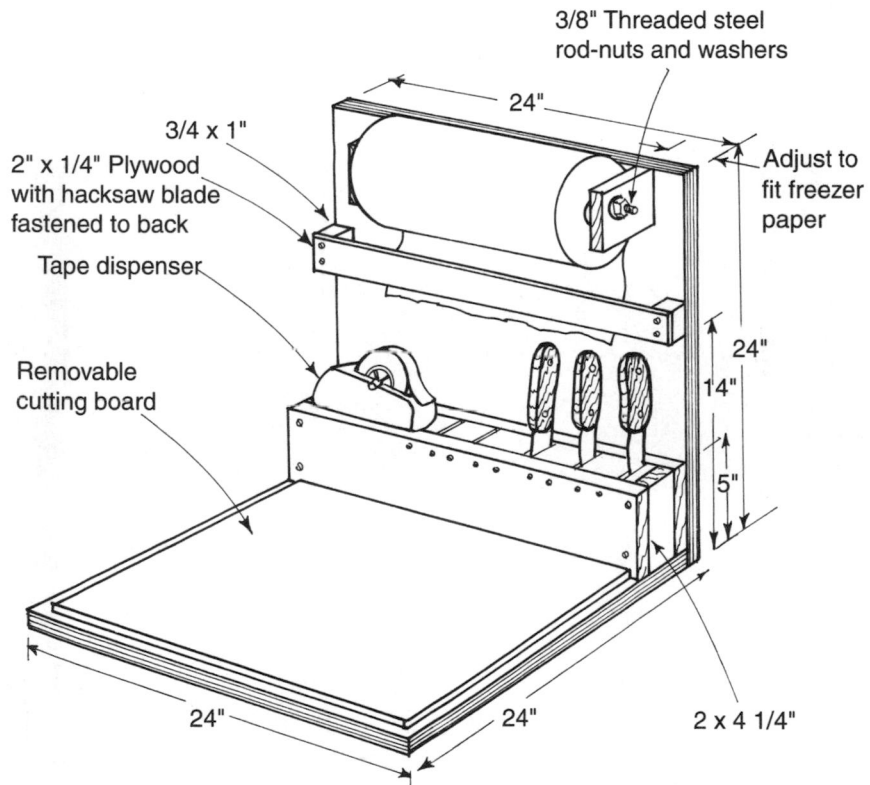

A butcher's tool holder can make butchering chores easier.

and it's covered with plastic laminate for easy cleanup. A butcher organizer such as the one shown can also be a great help in cutting and wrapping meat.

Most big game benefits from hanging or rapid cooling. A reach-in or walk-in cooler can be an invaluable addition to a butchering operation if a number of carcasses are handled, especially in hot climates. Many hunting camps use recycled refrigeration truck bodies, converting them to 110 volts or, in some cases, utilize generators to run them. Several commercial coolers are also available from Game Locker, including some small reach-in as well as some larger walk-in models. The smaller models will hold two to four deer, whereas the larger will hold up to twenty deer.

In Missouri, where we live, the deer season can range in temperature from below freezing to the 90s. I try to hang the carcasses in my barn if the temperatures are low enough. During hot weather, however, I use an old side-by-side refrigerator with all the shelves removed for the chore. The carcass is quartered and hung on hooks in the refrigerator. Most larger refrigerators will hold a

A cooler for hanging game, such as the unit shown from Game Locker, can be invaluable in hot climates. A small covered skinning and butchering shed can also make chores easier. (Photo courtesy Game Locker)

full carcass in this manner. You can also further cut the pieces down into backstrap, hindquarters, and front shoulders for hanging in limited space.

Game Locker also carries stainless-steel worktables, butcher block worktables, meat hooks, meat trees, meat saws, scales, and gambrels. Another excellent source for game-processing and butchering products is L.E.M. Products, Inc.

A good portion of most venison and big game goes into ground meat, and a quality grinder is a must. Hand-cranked grinders can be used for the chore, but they must be good-quality meat grinders, not economical kitchen grinders. If you intend to make sausages, you need a grinder with two blades: a ⅜- and a ³⁄₁₆-inch blade, or a ⅜- and a ¼-inch blade. Electric grinders are also available in various sizes, depending on the amount of meat to be ground. These range from about 2 pounds per minute up to 5 pounds per minute for commercial-grade models. I've tested a model from the Sausage Maker and found it excellent. Similar grinders are available from L.E.M., Cabela's, and Bass Pro Shops.

A good portion of venison is made into ground meat or sausage. A quality meat grinder is a necessity. A hand grinder can be used, but a powered grinder such as the heavy duty unit shown from Cabela's makes short work of the chore.

I was lucky enough to inherit an old grinder my granddad had. He actually ran it off the back wheel shaft of a Model A. My dad adapted a big horse motor to it. "Better not have your tie in the grinder when you turn it on," was granddad's favorite saying. It really works great. Most of the newer grinders, however, not only come with a variety of blades but also sausage stuffers that allow you to grind and stuff sausages at the same time.

Another handy item is a good-quality electric food slicer. It's great for slicing large quantities of meat for jerky. Chef'sChoice has two excellent models. Their International Folding Electric Food Slicer Model 650 is a heavy-duty professional slicer that folds compactly for easy storage. It can also easily be taken to hunting camp. They also have their International Professional Model 640, a rugged slicer with a food carriage that retracts, allowing slicing of large roasts. Steaks, ribs, and other bony cuts require a meat band saw. These are relatively expensive, but you can sometimes find them at sales of grocery stores going out of business. Round steaks often require tenderizing, and a number of tenderizing products are available from L.E.M.

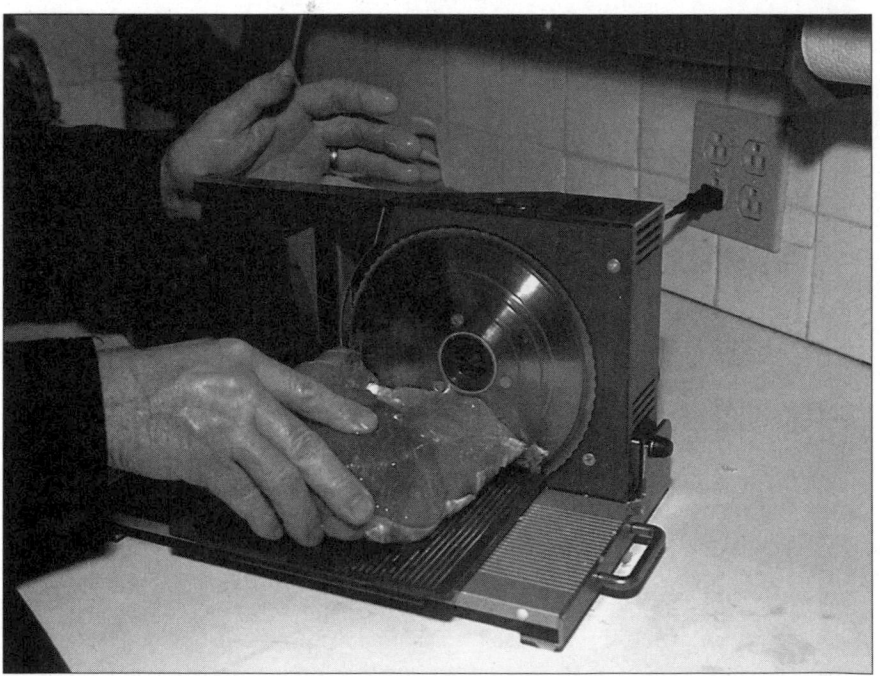

A vacuum packing system provides the best method for freezing venison.

Jerky is one of the favorite ways of using the tougher cuts of venison, and a dehydrator makes short work of drying jerky. We've used an Excalibur Dehydrator for a number of years—not only for jerky, but also to make fruit leathers and dried vegetables. You can make jerky in the traditional method of slicing the meat into thin strips. These days, you can also use a jerky machine that extrudes ground jerky meat into thin strips or rounds.

Venison is also popular in a variety of sausage cures. Mixes and equipment for sausage making are available from the Sausage

Smokers can be used to smoke jerky and sausages.

An electric food slicer, such as those from Chef'sChoice can be used for slicing jerky and thin steaks.

Maker, L.E.M., and Luhr Jensen. Luhr Jensen also has an excellent smoker, the Big Chief, that can be used to smoke the sausages.

A vacuum-packing system provides the best method of preparing meat for freezing, and we've extensively tested the FoodSaver Professional II from Tilia.

Field Dressing

Your deer is down. The first step is to approach the animal slowly and cautiously. Whether bowhunting or hunting with a gun, make sure you're ready for another shot when approaching the animal. Dead deer have been known to get up and run—or worse, attack the hunter. Approach the animal from behind, and poke or prod an eye with gun or bow to ensure the animal is dead. Once satisfied, the next step is to properly tag your deer.

Now you're ready for the field dressing. Proper field dressing can be one of the most important facets in providing tasty venison. In most instances, the quicker that field dressing is done, the better. This is particularly true in warmer climates. Field dressing a deer is not a hard chore and can be done in a matter of minutes once you learn how.

Unfortunately, several fallacies have been written concerning field dressing deer. Following some of the old hunters' tales can often cause more problems than they alleviate: for instance, cutting the animal's throat to allow for bleeding. Stockyard-killed animals are normally killed by stunning, and the heart pumps blood throughout the system for some time. These animals are "stuck" with a sticking knife through the chest into the heart to allow for fast bleeding, or their throats are cut. They are then usually skinned, or, in the case of hogs, sometimes scraped in hot water before they are gutted. This step may take some time. A gunshot that kills a deer, on the other hand, usually stops the heart by shock and provides adequate bleeding. A bow-taken deer is killed by loss of blood. In most instances, deer are gutted in the field very quickly after being killed. Cutting the throat of a deer is usually not necessary and will only expose meat to dust and dirt.

With the proper tools and a little practice, field dressing can be quick and simple. First step is to prop the deer up on its back.

Another common fallacy is that you should remove the scent glands from the hocks before field dressing. This not only is unnecessary, but you can contaminate the meat with a blade that has been used for the chore. I do like to remove the glands on hocks once the carcass is hanging, and then only with a knife used just for that purpose. These scent glands can be kept in a plastic re-closeable bag and used as a natural scent attractant for bucks. They can also be frozen and used the next season. Just don't forget to label them when you place them in your freezer, and make absolutely sure they are well wrapped.

The first step in field dressing is to put on disposable gloves, then roll the deer over on its back on a flat, smooth surface. If pos-

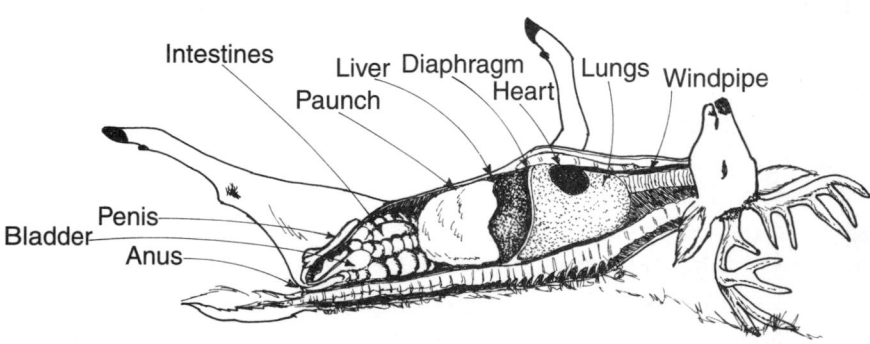

The location of the major organs.

sible, position the head slightly higher than the rest of the body. If field dressing must be done on a sloping area, such as a mountain-side, prop the animal in position with sticks, logs, or rocks.

Make a shallow, 2- to 3-inch cut to one side of the penis or the udder. Gently cut through the skin but not the inner intestine lining. You may wish to remove a buck's penis and scrotum at this time if allowed by law. Check local laws—some states require the genitals to remain on the field-dressed deer until the animal has been checked at a field station. If removing the genitals, slice them away from the skin, and allow them to hang back over the anus. Do not cut away from the rest of the viscera at this time.

Stand straddling the animal and face toward the head. Extend the index and second finger of your hand, palm up, into the shallow cut made in the skin and muscle. Position the knife blade edge up into the cut between your fingers. Carefully slit the belly muscle and skin from the beginning of the cut up to the sternum or bottom of the ribs. Keep the paunch pushed down with the back of your hand as you guide the knife blade with your fingers. A skinning knife with a gut hook makes this chore easy. Once the initial cut has been made, simply position the hook in place and pull toward the head of the animal. You will still need to hold the paunch down with your other hand.

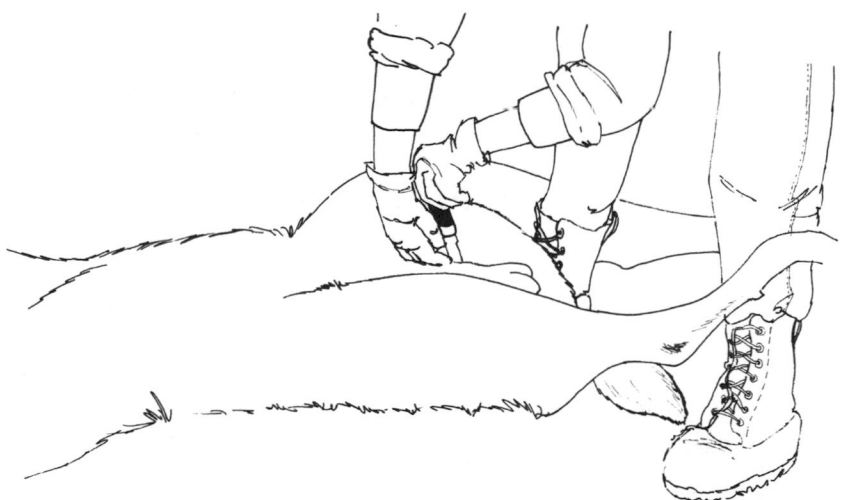

Make a shallow, 2- to 3-inch cut on one side of the penis or udder, cutting only through the skin.

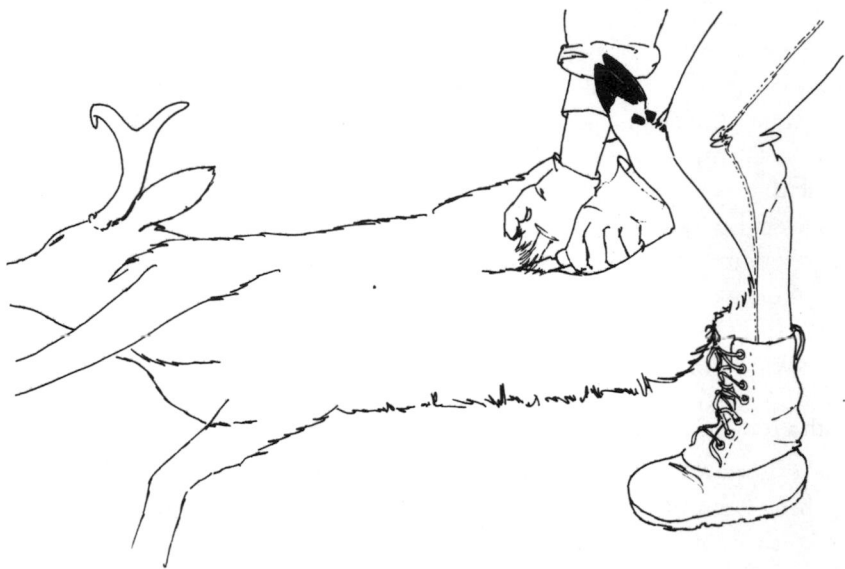

Continue the cut from the initial cut to the breastbone.

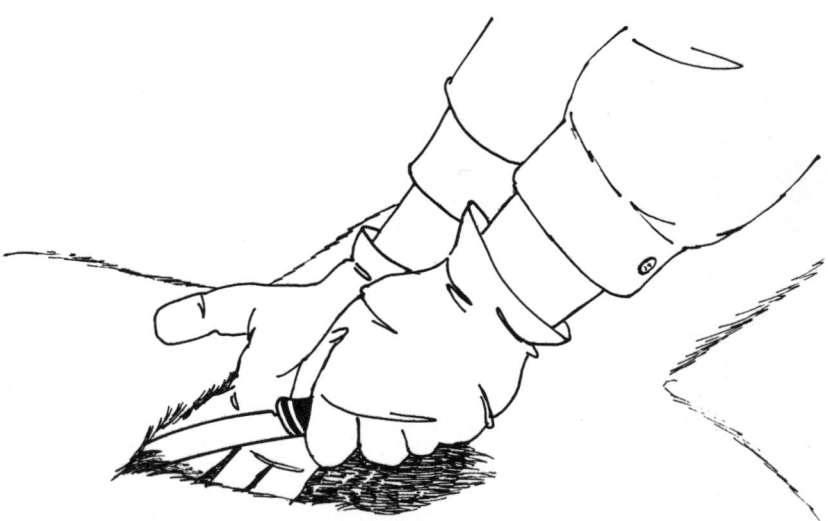

One way of making the cut is to use the back of your fingers to push down on the muscle of the paunch while holding the knife blade upward to make the cut.

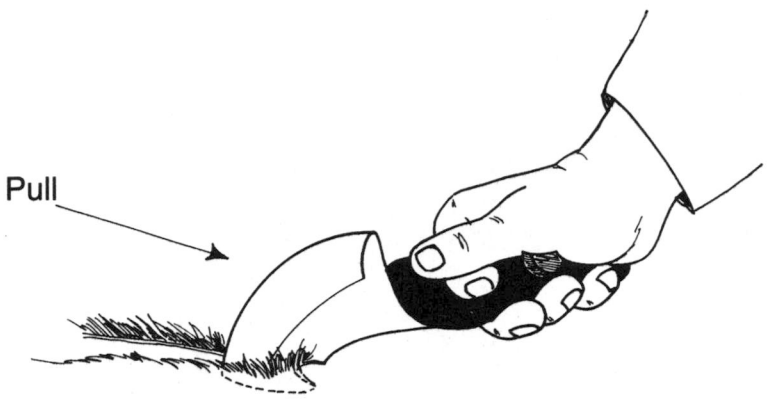

Pull

With a gut-hook knife you can make the cut quite easily.

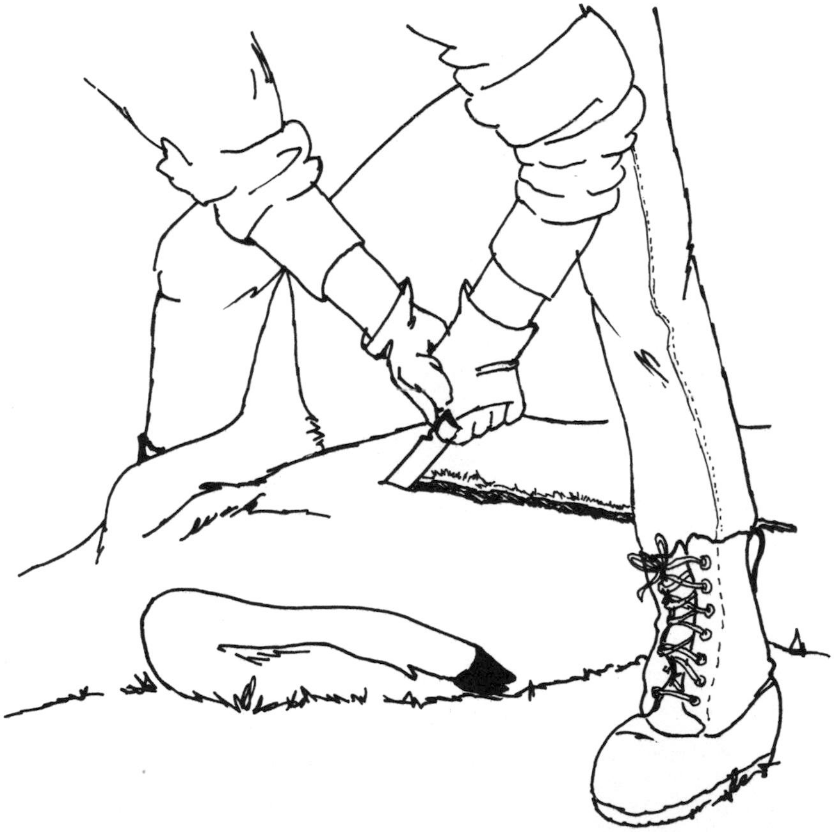

Cut through the breastbone or center of the rib cage. You can do this with a sharp, sturdy knife, game saw, hatchet, or knife with a saw-edged back.

The next step is to cut through the rib cage. Continue the cut through the cartilage of the centerline of the rib cage and up to the base of the neck. (Stop at the front of the chest if the animal is a trophy to be caped.) This cut can usually be made with a heavy-bladed knife, holding the knife blade up and pointed away from you, but it does take pressure. Another tactic is to position the blade angled downward and tap it with a rock or other heavy object to force it to "chop" through. You can also use a packable meat saw, camp hatchet, or knife for this task. If the animal is not a trophy to be caped, cut up to the throat.

Move to the rear of the animal and, using the point of a sharp knife, make a cut completely encircling the anus and vaginal opening of a doe. Push the knife blade through the pelvic opening and cut, much like coring an apple. Pull the rectum outside the body, and tie it off with a small cord to prevent feces from contaminating the meat during the rest of the field dressing. Now you can simply push the rectum tube back through the pelvic arch and into the body cavity to be removed with the rest of the intestines. Or you can split the pelvic arch. This will have to be done before hanging and actually makes for easier gutting. The first is the simplest if you

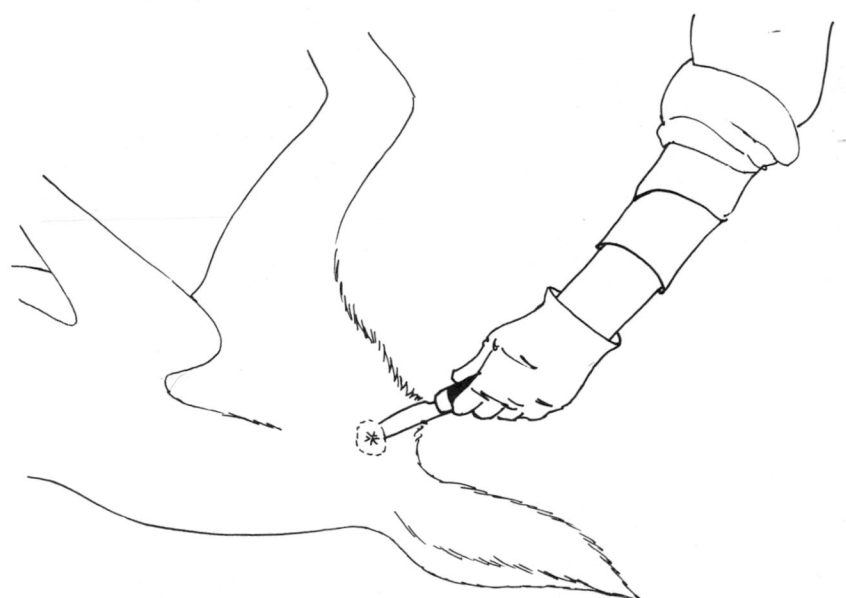

Using a sharp knife, make a cut encircling the anus and intestine.

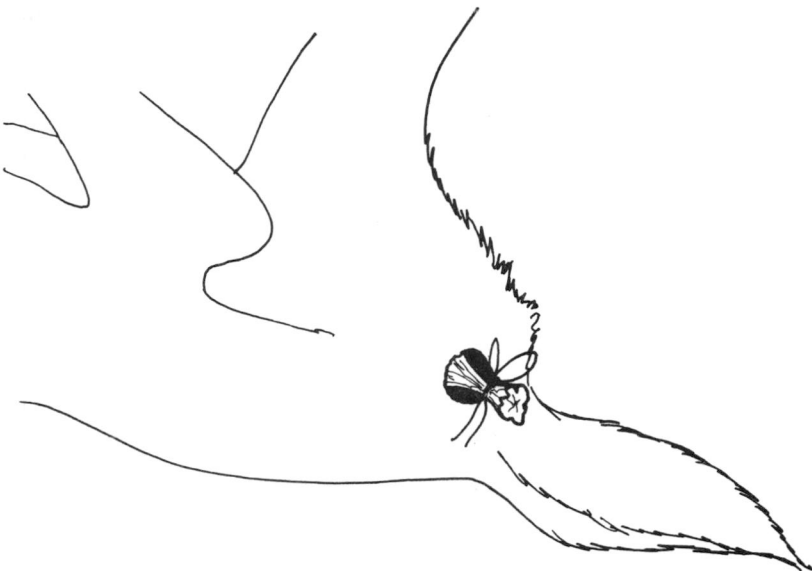

Then pull out the anus and tie it off with a piece of string.

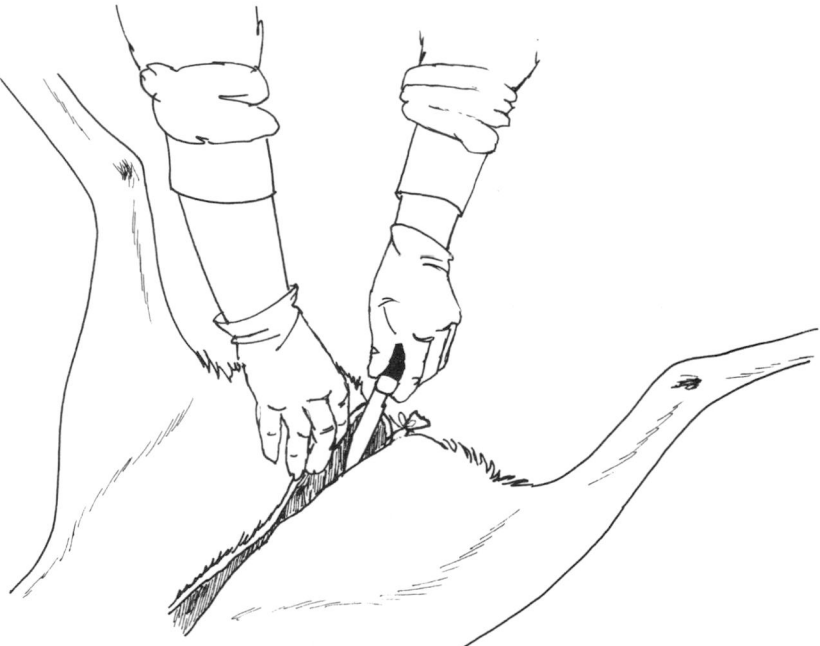

Cut through the thin muscle over the pelvic bone to locate the white line in the center of the bone. Then cut the pelvic bone with a knife, game saw, or hatchet.

don't have tools for splitting the arch. Splitting the arch, however, is the cleanest, and allows for quicker cooling.

To split the pelvic arch, locate the exact center of the hams, directly over the rectum, and slice through the inside of the hams until you reach the bone. You'll see a faint white line in the exact center of the pelvic arch. Press down on that with the knife to force the bone apart. Again, this may take some pressure, and a large knife is necessary. A hatchet can also be used for this chore, as well as a saw. Once the cut is made, push down on both legs. The arch will break with a snap, leaving an open channel to remove the rectal tube. Grasp the string-tied anus and tube and pull it up and outward.

Step to the head of the animal and grasp the gullet, pushing the material in it forward, then cut off the gullet and windpipe. Roll the carcass over on its side; the intestines and paunch will simply roll

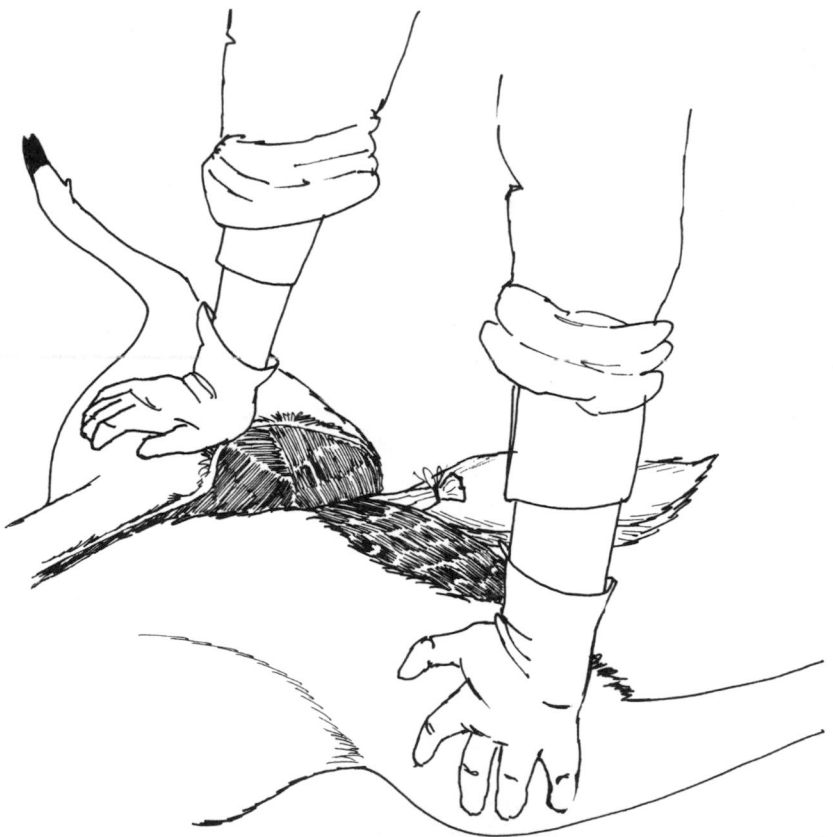

Push down on both legs to "snap" the pelvic arch apart.

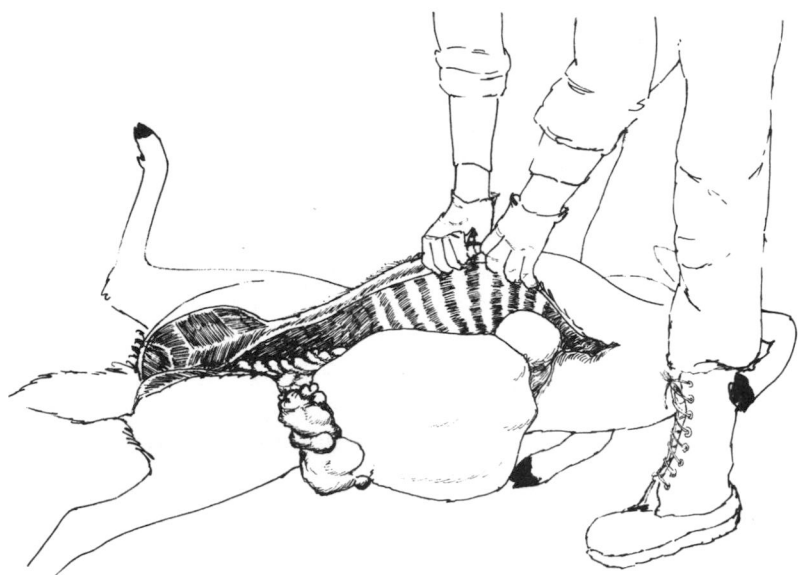

Lift the side of the carcass or roll it over. The paunch and entrails will spill out.

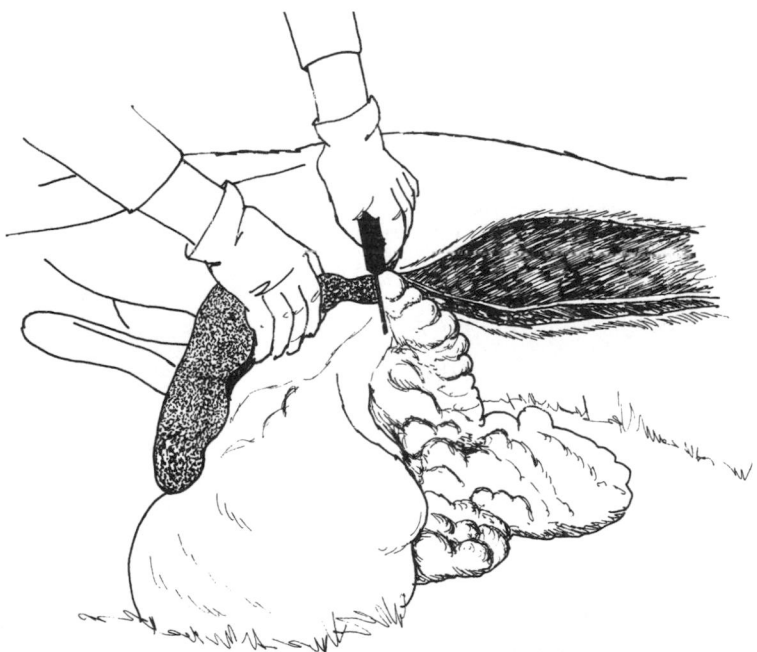

You will have to cut the diaphragm to remove the upper organs from the chest. Then cut the windpipe. Remove the liver, hoist the carcass up by the head, and allow the blood and fluids to drain out.

outward but will still remain attached with the diaphragm. This is actually the hardest part of the field dressing. You must reach into the chest cavity and cut around the diaphragm to release the lungs and other organs in the rib cage and allow all the organs, including the paunch, to roll out of the body cavity. The loosened rectal tube will come out with the rest of the intestines.

Cut away the liver, being careful not to cut into the bile, a greenish sac attached to the liver. Cut away the heart, and place both the liver and heart in a plastic bag.

Remove as much of the blood from inside the cavity as possible by lifting the head and propping the head high. If water is available, wash the blood from inside the cavity and prop the chest cavity open with a stick. Now you're ready to transport the animal from the field to camp or home.

HAULING OUT YOUR DEER

You've been chasing a big buck for almost a week. Finally he makes a mistake, and he's down. When you reach the animal, you realize not only is his rack impressive, he's huge and, of course, at the bottom of a ravine. You suddenly realize a daunting chore faces you. How are you going to get the critter out of the woods?

You have many options, depending on what type of equipment you have, whether you have help available, and where the carcass is located. In many instances, the simplest method is to drag out the carcass by hand. It is, however, the hardest on you. In fact, deer hunters have heart attacks each year from the effort. The method used in dragging can make a difference in how much effort is required. Grabbing on a buck's antlers and pulling is just about the least effective method. If you have to do the chore alone, a deer-dragging harness, such as those available from Hunter's Specialties or San Angelo All-Luminum Products, makes the chore easier. The harness puts the strain evenly on your shoulders and back. Many of today's tree-stand safety harnesses, such as the Strongbuilt Safe-Mate Harness, can also be used as a shoulder harness for deer dragging. You'll also need about 8 feet of nylon rope. Create a "halter" of the rope over the deer's neck and nose; this will pull the head and antlers up and away from the ground.

A buddy can be a great help. Two are much better than one, but again, a little special tactic can make the chore easier. Take the time to cut a pole long enough that two can grasp and pull. Create the pulling halter for the deer's head, tie the opposite end of the rope to the center of the pole, and two can pull with the pole in front of them quite easily.

A travois was used by native Americans to transport game carcasses. You can build your own travois from saplings, tie the carcass in place, and tote it out. An easier method than dragging or building

The next step is to transport the carcass out of the woods. The time honored method is to drag out the animal.

a travois is to use a sled. Any solid-bottom, plastic child's sled can be used for the chore and will slide over the ground easier than dragging the animal by itself. A couple of commercial products designed for the purpose include the Deer Sleigh'r from Cabela's and the Curlee Corporation Deer Glide from Bowhunters Discount Warehouse. Both units have grommets that can be used to lash the deer in place. Although it makes the chore easier for one, two makes dragging out a fairly easy chore.

The next step up from dragging is the use of wheeled carts. Warren & Sweat, well-known makers of quality tree stands, have three different models available through Cabela's. These not only make transporting game out of the woods easier, even in rough terrain, but they protect the meat and hide from dirt and damage. They are convenient and collapsible for easy transportation and storage. Off-road rubber balloon tires with heavy-duty steel rims provide go-anywhere ability. Three adjustable nylon web cargo tie-down straps secure the carcass in place. The unique design of the units balances the load weight over the heavy-duty axles, with zero weight at the handle. The Pony model handles up to 250 pounds and the Horse

Lightweight deer-hauling carts are also available these days for hauling out carcasses. (Photo courtesy Charlie's Horse)

up to 500 pounds. The Llama is a lightweight folding aluminum game cart that you can backpack in. Entire cart and wheels fold up into a camo backpack. The unit assembles on site in less than 2 minutes, weighs 20 pounds, and carries up to 250 pounds.

Brent Hunt's Trophy Whitetail Deer Hauler, available from Bass Pro Shops, is also a lightweight aluminum model that folds into a compact 24 × 38 × 6-inch size. For easy storage, the wheels can be removed to place the unit behind a vehicle seat. The unit carries a 300-pound load with ease and includes two cam-buckle straps to secure the game to the carrier. The hauler weighs just 11 pounds and has a 12-inch ground clearance.

Cabela's has its own version: the Super Mag Hauler. Featuring puncture-proof tires, the 24 × 82-inch platform provides plenty of room and helps distribute the weight evenly. It carries up to 550 pounds and folds down for easy storage and transport.

From API comes the Grand Slam Dolly. Folding, with spoked wide-track wheels, the unit uses an all-welded frame construction surrounding a unique rugged net-mesh bed with a 300-pound load capacity. The unit assembles in seconds with API's Quick-Clip pins. The Grand Slam Dolly extends to a full 79-inch length and collapses to a compact 51 × 24 × 2 inches for super-easy transportation. It weighs just 17 pounds.

The Multi Cart from Working Class Products features 13½ inches of ground clearance and has a 300-pound capacity. It folds to easily fit in a vehicle and can also be used with an ATV.

The Roleez Hunteez is a one-wheeled cart that glides on a cushion of air to roll easily over soft or uneven terrain with loads weighing up to 200 pounds. Constructed of ⅛-inch thick aluminum tubing, the cart collapses for easy storage and transport and weighs only 22 pounds. During loading, a retractable, U-shaped leg provides stability. Four polypropylene straps with stainless-steel buckles secure equipment or game to a loading tray. The load is centered over the wheel to minimize lifting while pushing or pulling. The secret to the cart's ability to glide is the exclusive Roleez wheel. Manufactured of puncture-resistant flexible plastic, it is inflated to only 3 pounds per square inch. This pliable tire spreads out under the load to distribute the weight over a wide area.

The Hunter's Moon Bucktruck is a one-wheeled cart featuring a no-flat tire that allows one or two hunters to maneuver the unit over a variety of terrain. It also doubles as a camp table.

Charlie's Horse Game Cart can carry a payload of 300 pounds. It collapses into a self-contained compact unit weighing 25 pounds and is easily transported within the carry bag/backpack.

Of course, I've discovered that the easiest method of hauling out game is with your ATV. I've used my Kawasaki Prairie 400 4 × 4 to haul out a number of deer quite handily. If you're not concerned about damaging the hide or antlers, as in the case of some does, you can simply hitch a rope to the deer's head and drag the carcass out of the woods. It's fast and easy; however, you can easily damage antlers and you will probably rub the hair off the hide. Dragging in a deer sled is one answer. Another is to place the carcass on the ATV. Make sure you don't overload your unit's capacity, and it does take some effort to get the carcass up on the ATV racks. This task can be made much easier with a number of products on the market that lift the big game onto your ATV. One is the Original DeerLift hoist. It mounts onto your ATV and allows you to easily lift the carcass up and onto the ATV.

One of the more interesting hoists is the Pa-Paw's ATV Game Hoist. This unit has a two-piece telescoping vertical shaft and a

These days ATVs are often used to haul deer out of the woods. They make the chore quick and easy.

A number of hoists are available that make loading a deer on an ATV easy, even for the lone hunter. (Photo courtesy Professional Hunting Products)

horizontal boom. The unit fits into a bracket that can be attached to either the rear or front of your ATV. A manual winch completes the unit, which can very quickly be disassembled and stowed for transportation or storage. The hoist boom can be extended to 8 feet and has a 300-pound capacity when extended to 7 feet. A two-position support leg, which is adjustable to any ground-level condition, is fitted into a mounting bracket that stabilizes the unit and prevents the ATV from overturning when hoisting game up. The Pa-Paw's ATV Game Hoist offers double for your money. It can be used to hoist the game onto your ATV for transportation or as a hoist to hang the carcass for field dressing or allowing the body cavity to cool and drain.

A number of utility vehicles also make hauling out deer simple and easy. These are basically ATVs configured to seat two people with a cargo bed in the back. Some even come with an electric dump bed. Add a winch, and it's easy to get even the biggest deer up in the vehicle bed for easy transportation. These include the Kawasaki Mule, E-Z-Go WorkHorse, Club Car Pioneer, John Deere Trail Gator, Polaris Ranger, and Pug Power models.

An easier and safer method is using a trailer behind your ATV to transport the game animal. You can transport larger animals than you can safely carry on your ATV, and it's also easier on your ATV. Most ATV manufacturers offer carts or lightweight trailers that can be used behind their units for transporting gear to camp, hauling tree stands around, and getting your game out of the woods when you're successful. Some lightweight trailers made for lawn tractors can also be used, but most aren't rugged enough or don't have the heavy-duty, off-road tires required for backwoods work.

The Warren & Sweat Kangaroo ATV trailer, which is available from Bass Pro Shops, is an excellent example. It has a cargo space of more than 5 cubic feet and will haul 500 pounds over mild terrain or 350 pounds over uneven or rough terrain. It features solid, 20-inch nonpneumatic tires, creating a 10-inch ground clearance.

One of the best we've seen is the Tag-A-Long from Trax America. It will carry two of your hunting buddies and all their gear in comfort. It features ATV tires for a comfortable ride, a splash shield to prevent mud from reaching passengers, and a large cargo area that can be used to haul gear and game.

The HuntMaster from Robco Manufacturing is a combination ladder stand and big-game dolly. It is 14 feet high as a tree stand and has a 500-pound capacity. It also has an optional ATV hitch or optional hitch hauler for truck bumpers.

Quite often, big-game animals go down in tricky terrain—off steep bluffs, at the bottom of ravines, in brushy tangles and saplings so thick you can't crawl through, as well as other places where extracting the carcass sometimes becomes a serious lesson in physics. In this case, a power winch quickly becomes an absolute "must" tool. Electric winches mounted on your pickup, SUV, or ATV can save the day. Many ATV manufacturers offer winches as an option to their machines. For instance, Kawasaki features a Warn A2500 winch and a couple of mounts available for their ATVs.

Rule vehicle winches are a prime example of the vehicle winches available, featuring lifetime lubrication, free spool, a long cable, power in or out, weather-tight construction, positive braking, and three-stage planetary gearing. They're available in six series, ranging from 1,400-pound, single-line rating stall to 8,400 pounds, cable lengths from 50 to 100 feet, and in both 12- and 24-volt models.

In some cases, you simply can't get a vehicle or ATV near the downed animal, and that's where the portable winches—such as the new Rule line—offer go-anywhere pulling power. In Maine last year, I watched as hunters easily winched a 1,000-pound moose across an almost impossible labyrinth of fallen trees, the only route to the animal. The Rule gasoline-powered Model G-1800E winch uses a very dependable Echo Power Head (chain-saw style). The unit uses Echo's extremely reliable Rapid-Reply Starter System and hauls as much as 1,800 pounds on a single line and 3,500 pounds on a pulley block line. Simply anchor it to a tree or other secure object and start pulling. Ground anchors are also available as optional accessories.

When selecting a winch for lifting or pulling an object, the single-line stall rating should be at least twice the weight of the object being lifted. Additional layers of cable on the drum (one layer on top of the other) reduces pulling capacity. There is about a 10 percent reduction in capacity per layer on the drum.

To increase pulling capacity, an optional pulley block or double line can be used. This will increase line pull by approximately 85 percent.

Don't break your back and risk a heart attack with your big buck. There are plenty of safe and easy ways of hauling out your deer.

Back at camp or home, soak the heart and liver in several changes of water, then hang the liver in a safe place to dry for a short period of time. If in hunting camp, the traditional meal of the first animal is liver. Prepared properly, it's delicious.

CHAPTER

3

Hanging and Skinning

HANGING

The next decision is whether to hang the animal for aging, and that decision depends on a number of factors. If you live or hunt in hot climates, the single best thing you can do is get the carcass to a slaughterhouse or cooler as quickly as possible. In many instances, slaughterhouses won't hang or age venison. If you don't have a cooler and are doing the work yourself, skin and butcher the animal as quickly as possible, and do the chore in a cool shady place.

Studies done by Joyce A. Hosch and Milo Shult for Texas A & M reveal that aging the carcass created more tenderness. The aging process not only retards and extends rigor but tends to increase the water-holding capacity of the meat, both of which are helpful in the tenderizing process.

Taste testers discovered overall satisfaction to be a combination of the desired traits. During the test demonstration, the group of animals showing the highest overall satisfaction were female animals aged 1 week. Hosch and Shult discovered that boning the hams before aging decreased tenderness. This is due to the fact that the bone serves as muscle attachment. When the bone is removed, the muscles, which are in an unnatural state, are allowed to contract more because there is no attachment; therefore, tenderness is reduced.

In cool climates (temperatures staying below 45 degrees F), and if you intend to do the slaughtering yourself, you can allow the carcass to hang either at camp or home. Hang the carcass in a barn, shed, or garage, making sure it is high enough to be out of reach of

If the weather is cool enough, or you have a cooler, hanging the carcass for a few days can increase the tenderness and "flavor."

cats, dogs, and varmints. I've found it best to skin the carcass as quickly as possible. Several years ago, I hung a couple of deer just before a trip and left the skins on. The temperature was below freezing, and when I returned several days later, I attempted to skin the animals. I had to cut the hides away. The carcass will quickly harden on the outside, keeping the meat moist on the inside. If insects are present, you might prefer to cover the carcass with a cheesecloth game bag.

We have always hung the carcass for 7 to 10 days to allow for aging. Ideally, you should hang the carcass by the head to allow blood and fluids to drain out of the body cavity. The carcass should then be hung by the rear legs for skinning and quartering. Make sure the body cavity is propped open with a stick to aid in cooling.

Some seasons in Missouri—where we live—provide ideal aging weather, but most don't. The solution is fairly simple. An old refrigerator turned to 42 degrees F is used for the aging process when the weather is warm. The carcass is quartered and the quarters placed in the refrigerator. Because of the lack of air circulation, the meat should be turned frequently to prevent lying on one side continuously. (Stand the quarters on end to drain.) If you use the refrigerator method or have a cooler in which the meat can be hung, it's best to skin the carcass before hanging.

SKINNING

Skinning is easiest with the animal hanging, and as discussed in Chapter 1, a variety of means can be used to hang the carcass. I prefer to hang it by the hocks with the head down. Although an animal can be skinned hanging from the head, I've discovered it's easier using my method and a few shortcuts.

You can cut off the rear legs just below the hocks, but I prefer to leave them, as they provide easier handling of the hams after they're removed from the gambrel. Insert the point of a knife blade from the side opposite the scent glands in the hock area, and make a cut between the bone and tendon. Do this for each leg to create an opening for the gambrel. Insert the gambrel in place, and hoist the carcass up. I like to only hoist high enough that I can easily reach the rear legs and ham area at this time. Starting at the inside of one ham, make a slit in the skin up to just below the hock area

Cut

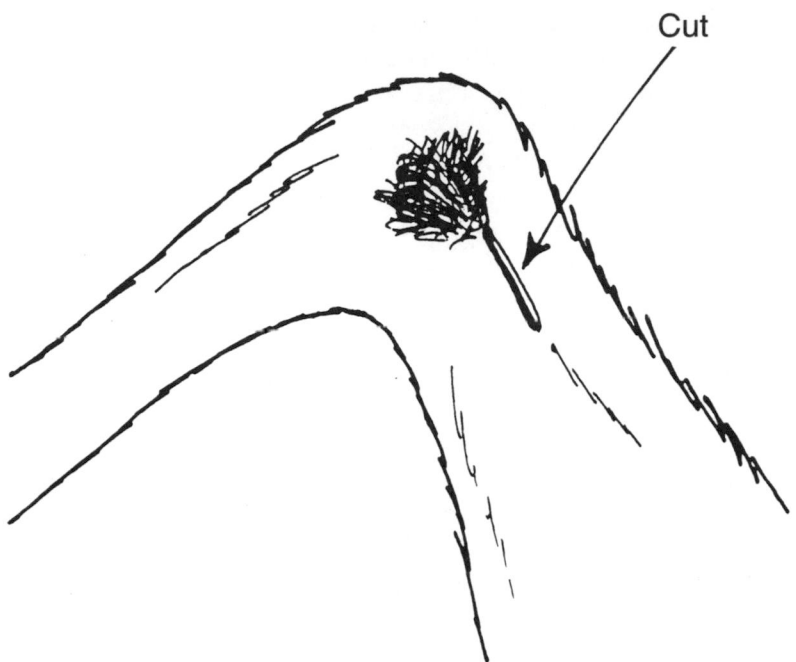

Skinning is done with the carcass hanging head down. The first step is to make a cut between the tendon and bone on the rear legs to insert the gambrel points.

containing the gambrel. Cut around the leg at this point, leaving skin in the hock and gambrel-point area. This portion of the leg contains almost no meat and is cut away during butchering.

During all skinning cuts, keep the knife blade pointed outward to avoid cutting hair. Loose or cut hairs are a problem on the carcass, and cutting from the hide out instead of down through the hair alleviates most of the problem. Pick off loose hairs as they appear, and keep a cloth around to wipe any hairs that accumulate on the knife blade. Follow this, and your butchering chores will be much easier and the meat more healthy and better in appearance.

Note: The following skinning process is for nontrophy animals. If the cape is to be kept for mounting, follow the caping information in Chapter 4.

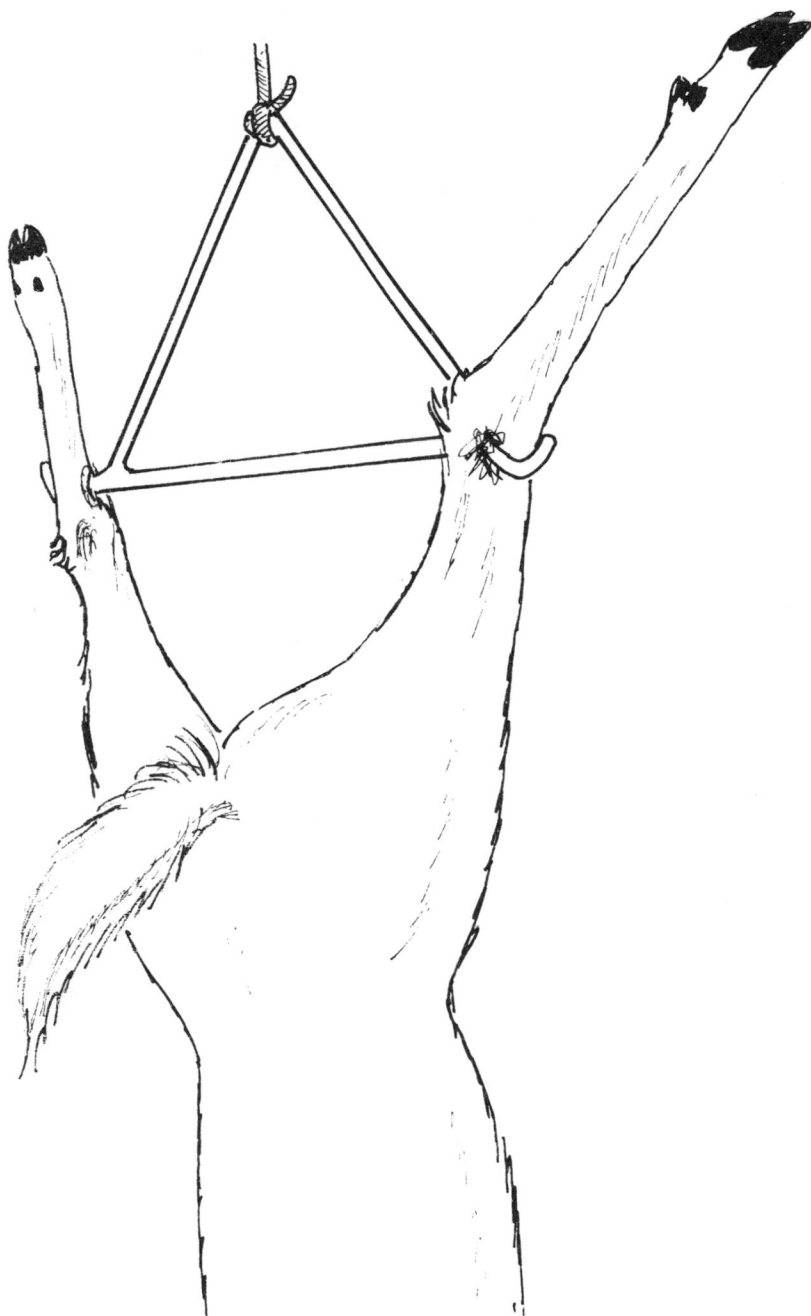

Hoist the carcass up on the meat pole with the hams at about eye level.

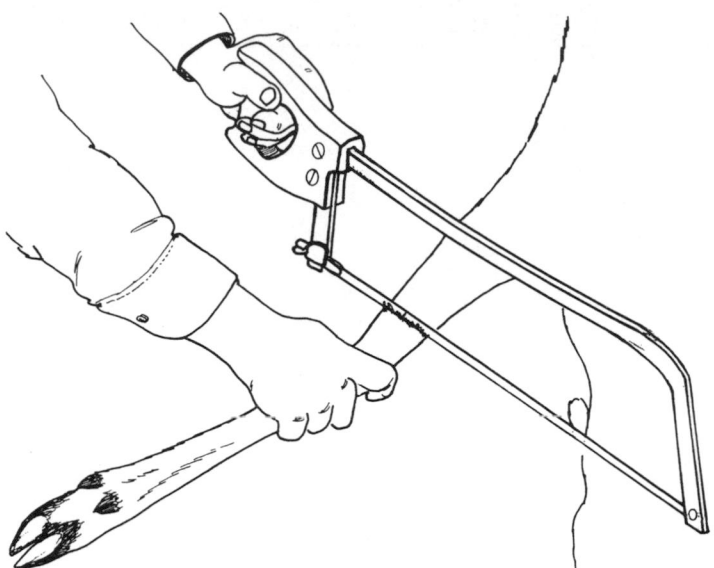

Saw off the front legs just above the joint.

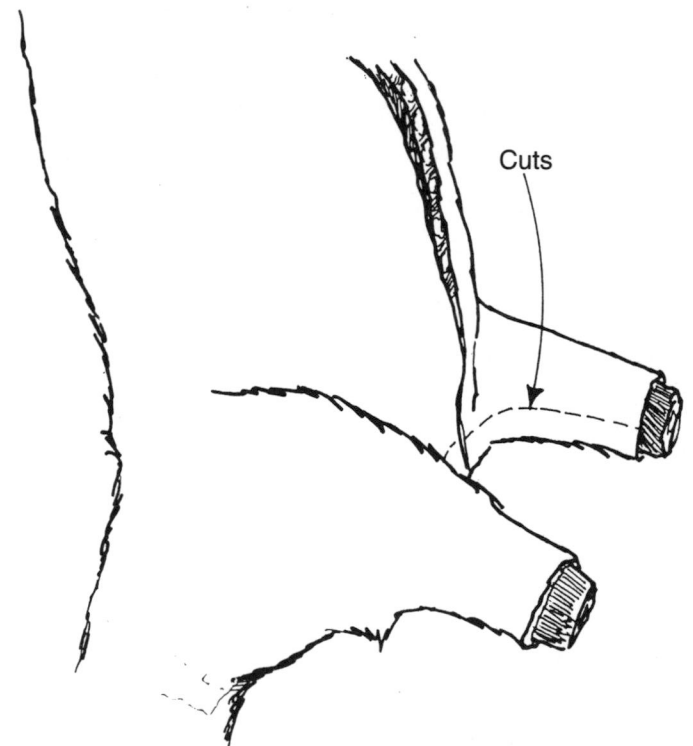

Cuts

To make skinning easier, skin out the front legs first.

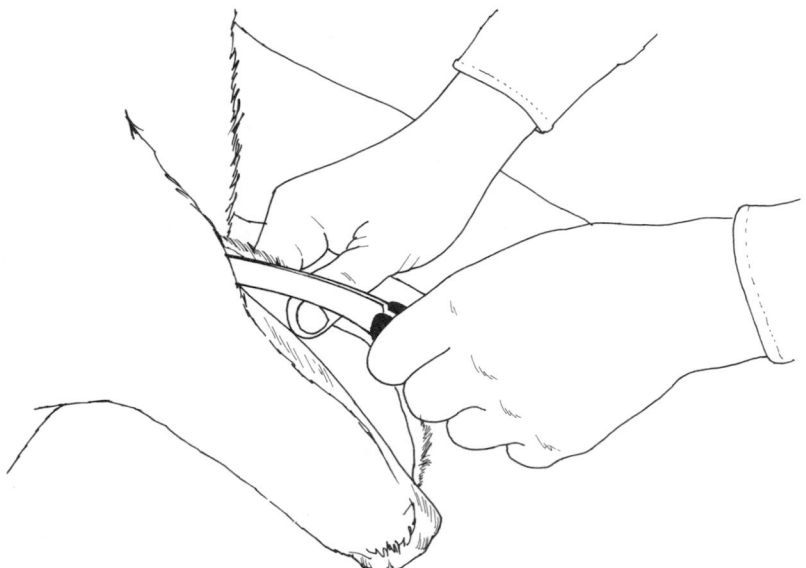

Make a cut from the cut-off leg with the knife blade facing up, along the backside of the leg.

Continue the cut across the chest to the cut at the end of the breast-bone or throat.

At this point I take a shortcut. Most wild-game skinning information is a copy of domestic meat skinning, but wild game is different. At this point, cut off the front legs just behind the knee joint. Then I use another trick. Make a cut in the skin on the inside of the legs from the cut-off leg ends to the center of the chest. Skin out the front legs to the shoulders. There's a reason for this step. As the hide is peeled off, it tends to drape down over the front legs, making skinning them at that time a chore. If they're done first, it makes skinning much easier.

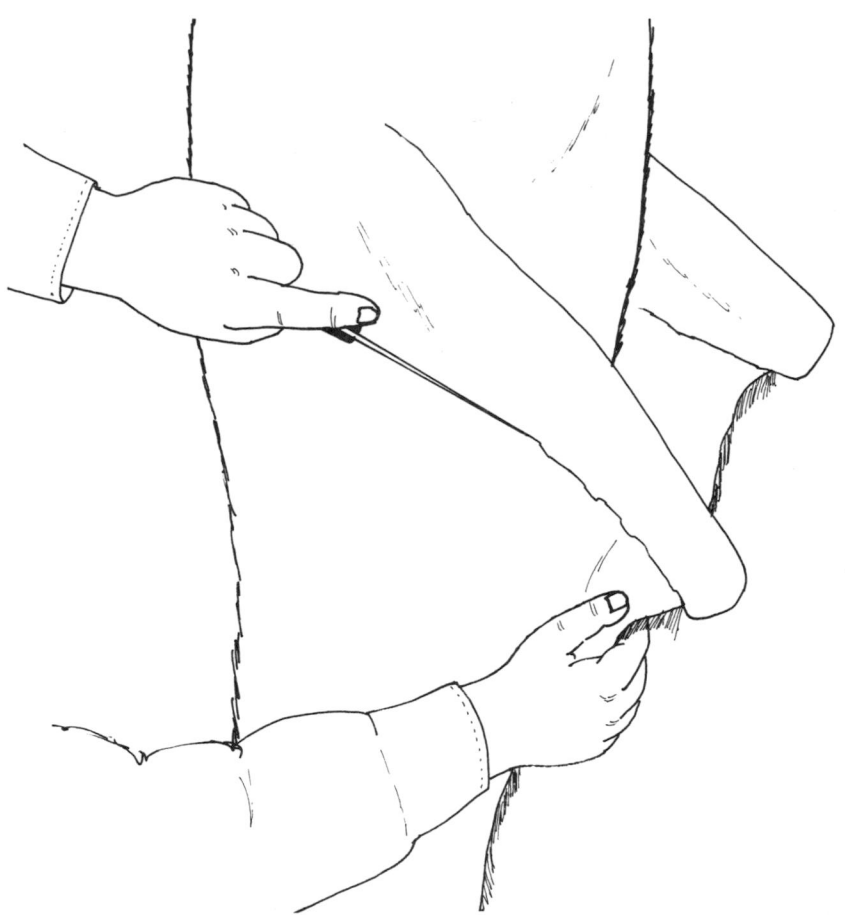

Peel out and skin the front legs and chest area.

Then go back up to the rear of the carcass and skin around the inside of the ham and the leg using the knife blade between the inside of the skin and meat to help remove the skin. Cut and pull at the same time. Do both hams down to the tail. Skin around the base of the tail to expose the bone, then cut off the tail with a meat saw or hand saw.

Move back up to the ham area and continue to cut and pull the hide down. Once you get the hide started on the back and sides, it can often be "fisted" or pulled down and away fairly easily. Use the knife to release the hide from the meat as needed. Try to leave as much meat on the carcass and off the skin as possible.

Once the skin drapes down around shoulders and front legs, continue to cut and pull it away from them. Continue pulling and cutting the skin, allowing it to drape down as you go to the base of

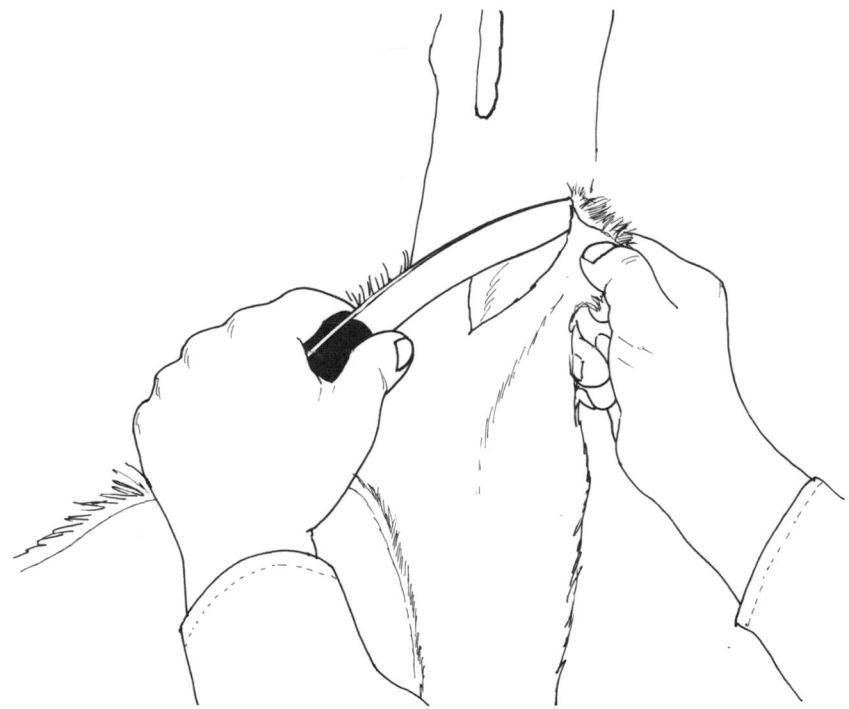

Then go back up to the rear legs, and with the skinning knife, blade pointed out, make a cut in the skin just below the hocks.

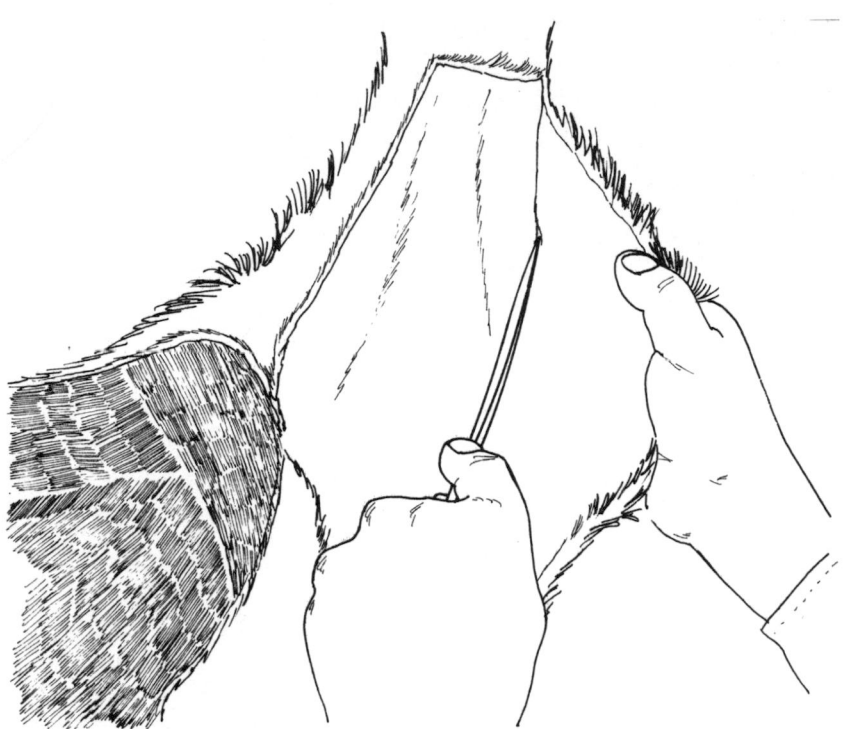

Peel the skin away from the leg and inside of the ham, using a sharp skinning knife to cut away stubborn areas.

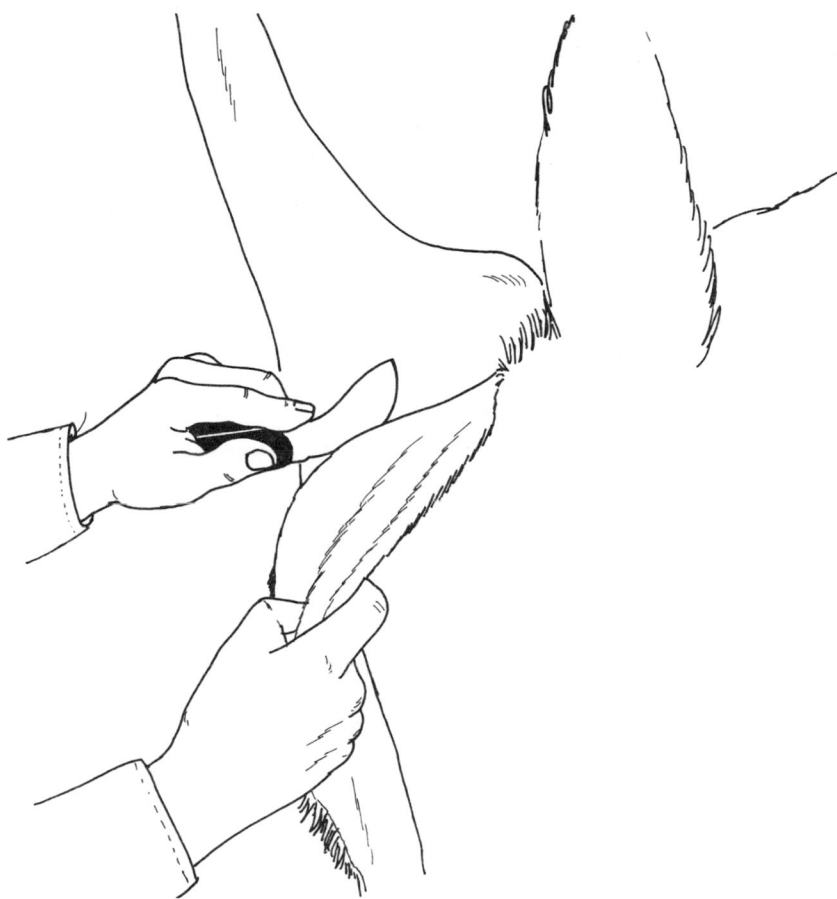

Work around the leg and ham, pulling the hide and cutting with the knife to release as needed.

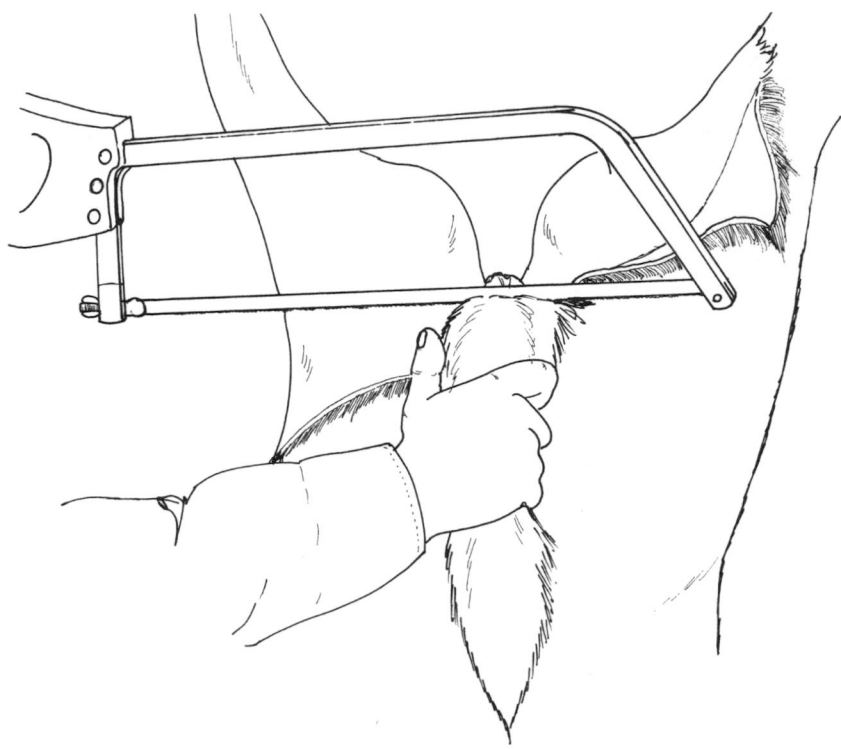

Once down to the tail, cut through the tailbone from the underside, leaving the tail on the skin.

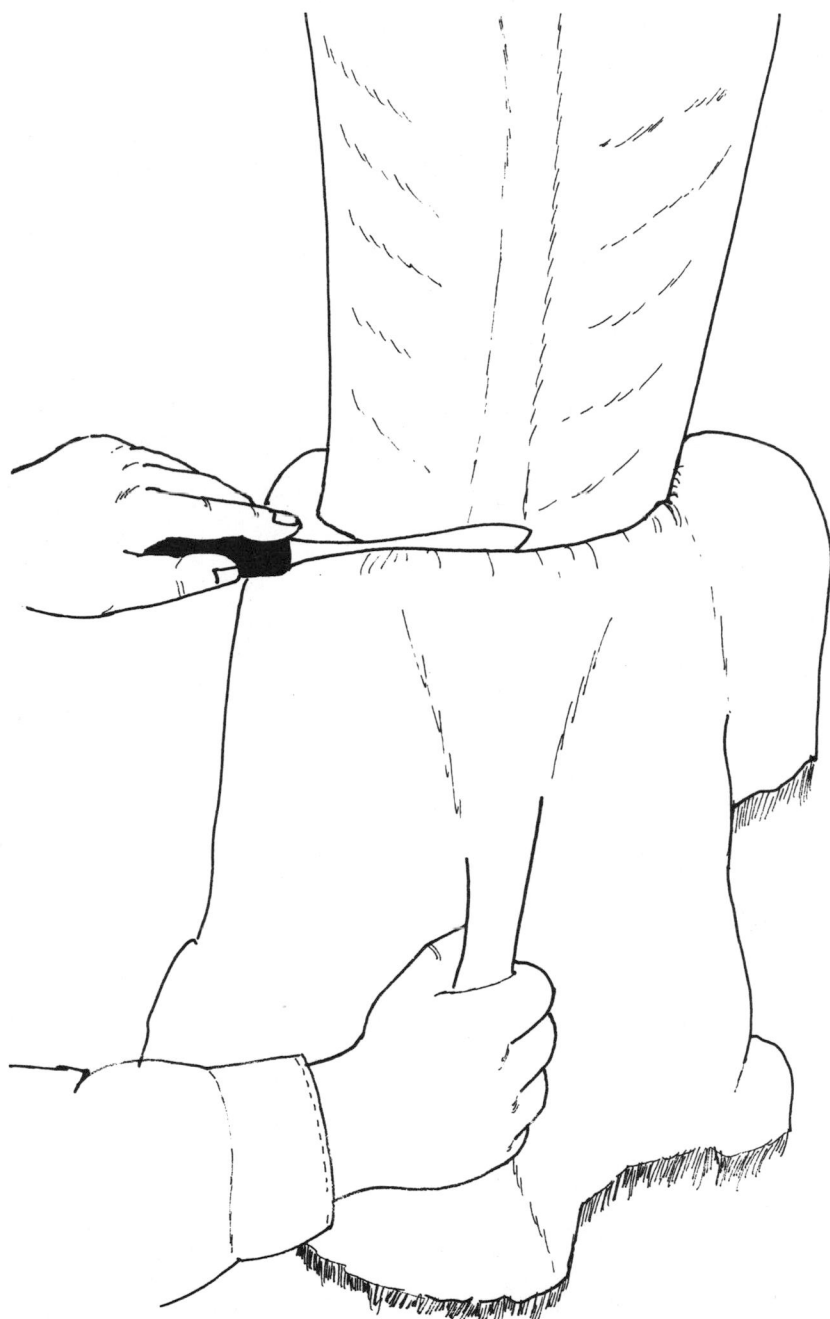

Continue peeling and cutting the skin away from the back, belly, and sides. In many instances the skin will pull away quite easily until you get to the shoulder area.

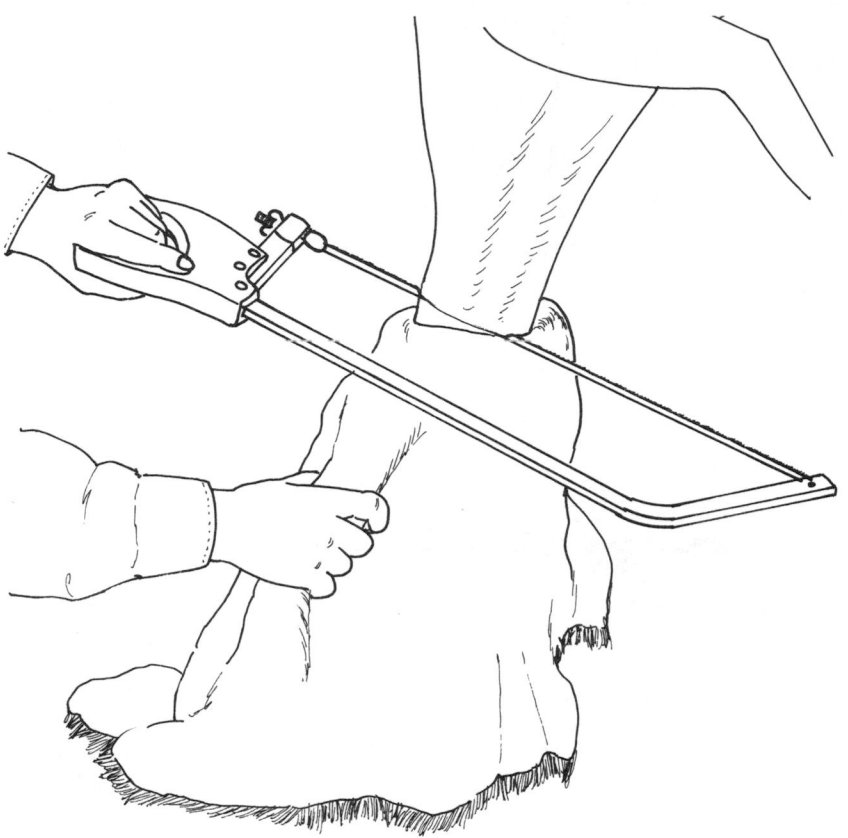

Skin down to the head and cut the head off.

the neck. You will probably wish to continue hoisting the carcass higher in order to make your work easier.

Cut the head off. This can be done with a sharp knife, slicing around the head and neck joint at the junction of jaw and neck. Then twist the head to release the bone connection. After the bone releases, cut the remaining muscle holding the head in place.

Carefully go over the entire carcass, and remove any hairs that might have adhered in the skinning process.

If you intend to keep the hide, cut the head away from it and salt the hide liberally. Roll the hide up hair side out. Take it to the tanner or taxidermist, or place it in your freezer until you can tan it yourself.

CHAPTER 4

Caping and Mounting

If you plan to keep the head of a trophy deer or other big game for mounting, the animal must be skinned differently than if you are simply keeping the meat. Proper skinning or caping in the field can make all the difference in a beautiful mount you can proudly hang on your wall or a terrible mount you're ashamed of or the taxidermist has to work unduly to mount. In the case of backpacking or horsepacking, in some instances, you may cape the animal and leave the skull in the skin until you get back to camp where you or the packer can continue the skinning. You may prefer to have the taxidermist do the final caping, or you may prefer to cape the animal right on the spot. This depends on a lot of factors, including how much time you have, the location where you are skinning, the weather, and the temperature.

If you are skinning to leave the skull in place in the hide, only four cuts are needed. How you make these cuts, however, is extremely important.

The first step toward proper caping begins in the field dressing. Do not cut the skin at the throat or split the breastbone while the skin is on the carcass. Remove the cape first. Most hunters don't leave enough of the skin for a proper mount, thinking only the neck in front of the shoulder is enough. The best tactic is to cut the cape starting behind the front shoulder and at the rear of the withers on the back of the animal. The first cut is from the withers, behind the front shoulder and down to the belly on each side, meeting and completely encircling the breastbone.

Then cut down the inside of the front legs to just above the front joint. Make a circle cut around the front legs. The next cut starts at the top of the withers and proceeds to the back of the skull behind the antlers, approximately between the ears. Part the hair,

A trophy animal for which you wish to have the head mounted is skinned in an entirely different manner.

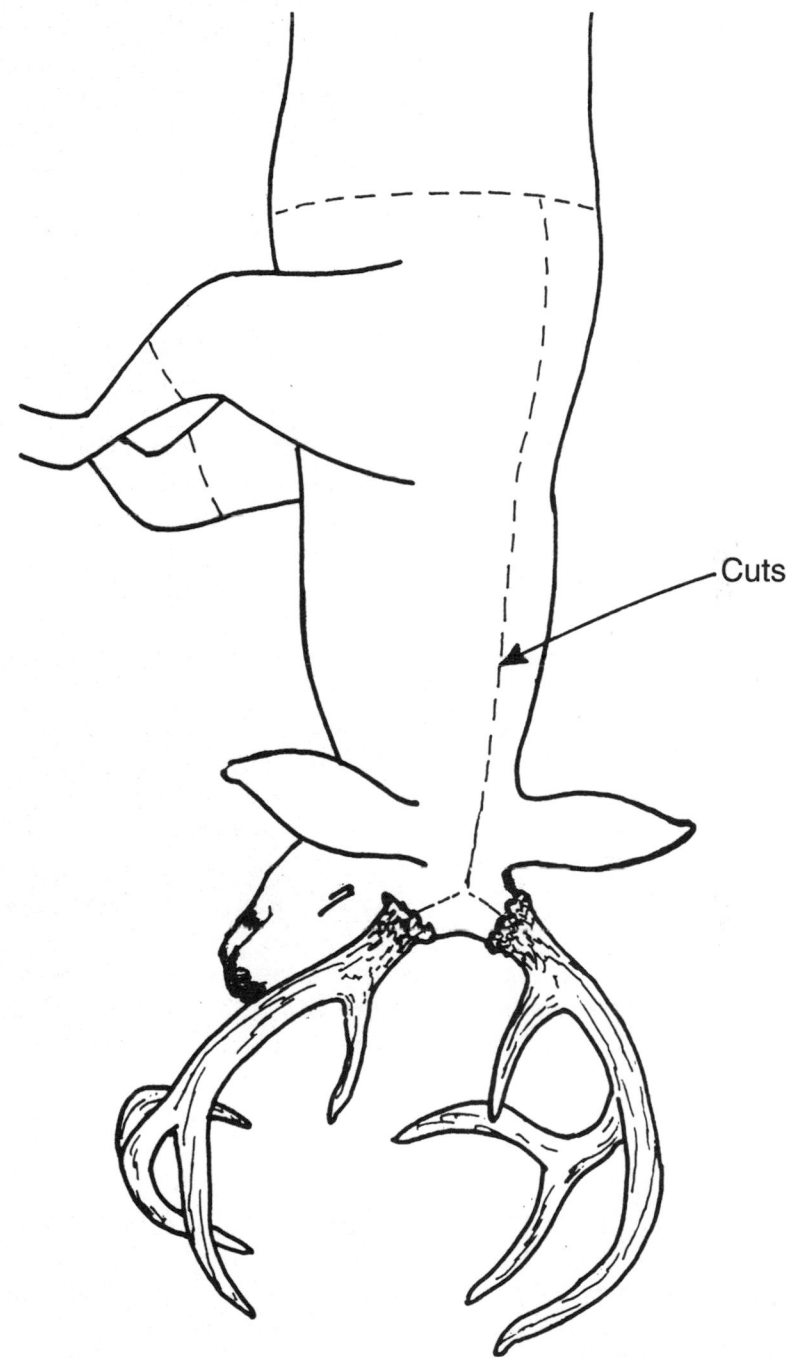

Dotted lines show the skinning cuts needed for caping a head for mounting.

and make this cut as straight and as smooth as possible. It's a good idea to make the cut from the inside to prevent cutting through the hairs on the top of the neck. This makes for a neater seam when sewn together by the taxidermist. Make sure you stop the cut before you get between the antlers. Then make a Y cut from the neck cut up to the rear of each antler base.

Pull the cape off, starting behind the shoulders and using the knife to loosen as needed. When you get to the joint of the neck and skull, remove the head. Pull the skin well forward of the area to be cut, and keep the skin out of the way so you don't accidentally cut it in severing the head from the carcass. Cut through the muscle over the large neck joint just behind the skull. Cut around the neck at this point. Bend the head back so you can expose the muscle and sinew that needs to be cut. Once all have been cut, you can twist off the head. Immediately salt the exposed head and skin. Most taxidermists prefer the cape to be delivered in this manner; however, this can be done only in cool weather. Remember to salt well in the eyes, ears, and nostril openings as well. This is all that needs to be done if the cape can be taken to the taxidermist within a few days.

If you can't get the cape and head to a taxidermist within a few days, you'll need to skin out the head as well. Many outfitters and guides prefer to cape out the head as they skin the animal, while the carcass is hanging on the meat pole. This can be done, but it's easier if you have the head and cape in one piece. You can then place the head and cape on an elevated surface or table for easier working.

Actually, caping in this manner is a fairly easy chore. I remember one time in a Texas hunting camp when I killed out early and had a couple of days of free time on my hands. I caped out my deer and then ended up caping out a couple more for my friends. It sure beat watching daytime television at the lodge. The main rule in caping is to take your time, work slowly, and pay attention to what you're doing. Other than that, caping is simple. You will need a good sharp knife, preferably with a relatively short but sturdy blade.

Start at the Y-cut and work toward the base of the ears and the burrs of the antlers. A rounded point knife is best for the next chore. With the skin folded back toward the antlers, cut upward underneath the "boss" of the antlers to remove the skin. A large, blunted, flat-bladed screwdriver can also be used to help push the

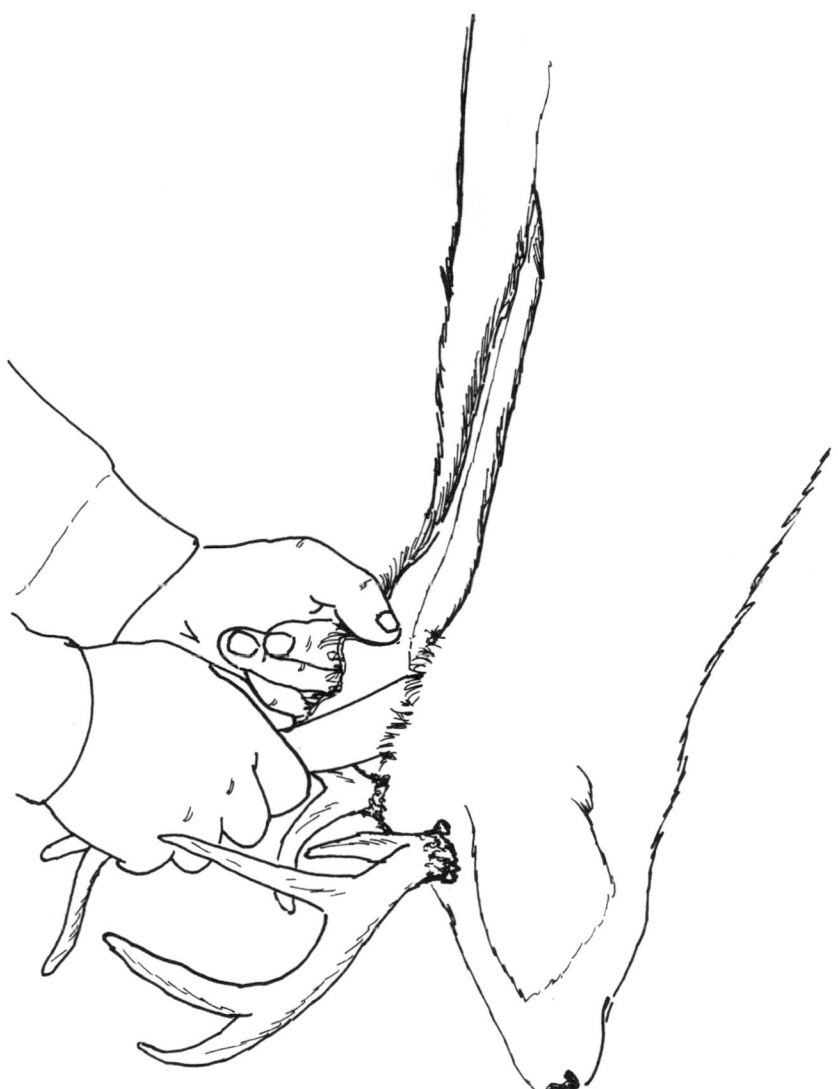

Make the cuts to remove the skin from the front portion of the deer, down to the head. Then cut the head off with the cape attached.

skin away from this area and is especially helpful on gnarly old trophy antlers. Make sure you don't slice through the skin at this point. Go around each antler very carefully, using the knife point to release and the screwdriver to push away until the skin clears the antlers.

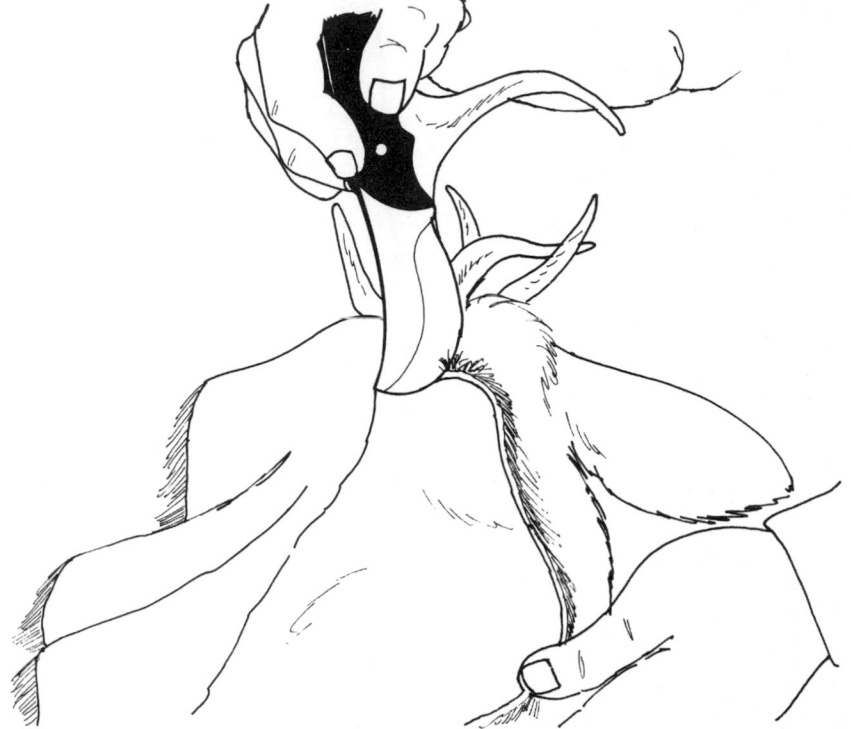

Place the head and cape on a sturdy work table and make the Y-cuts on the back of the head up to the base of each antler.

Once you've cleared the antlers, you've finished the hardest part, but not necessarily the most complicated. Continue skinning until you reach the ears. Once the yellow cartilage of the ears is visible, cut down and forward through this cartilage to the skull to free the ears. It's best to cut deep right at the base of the ears, as you can remove the flesh later on.

Continue skinning toward the eyes. Most beginners make their biggest mistake with the eyes. Take extra care not to cut the eyelids. They can not be easily repaired if accidentally cut. Prevention is the best cure. Cut toward the bone, away from the lid, and hold the skin taut as you work, until you reach the eye opening. Before you begin on the eyelids, insert your finger into the eye and below the outside of the eyelid. Pull the eyelid carefully and gently away from the skull, and at the same time, use your knife to cut the skin free from the eye socket. You can feel your knife blade under the

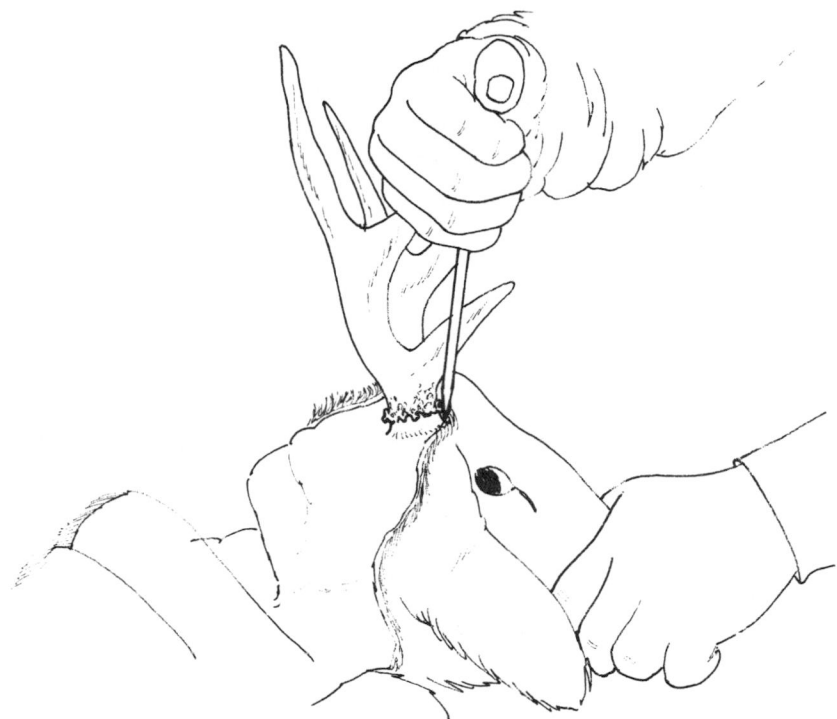

The skin is removed from under the antler burrs with a sturdy screwdriver prying the hide away.

skin as you work. Whitetail deer and other antlered game have a tear duct in front of the eyelid. The tear duct is firmly connected to the skull down in a small channel, and it must be carefully cut and pried out of the channel. Continue to keep the eyelid taut as you cut the tissue between the eyelid and bone until you reach the tear duct. Skin as close to the bone as you can to cut away the eyelid and tear duct.

Continue the skinning, using the knife to make little, short strokes down the bridge of the nose and along the sides of the jaw until you reach the corners of the mouth. Then insert your fingers into the mouth and pull away from the skull to pull away the lips. Cut the cheek muscles about three-quarters away from the corners of the mouth. This will be removed by the taxidermist.

Skin carefully and close to the bone on the underside of the jaw to free the lower lip. Make sure you don't cut through the lower lip at this point.

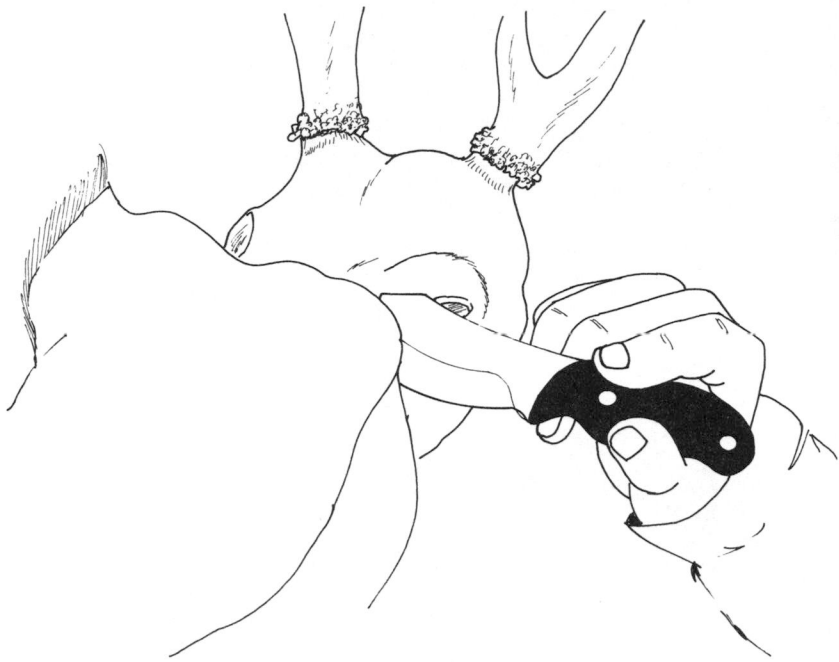

Continue skinning out the head. Cut very carefully around the eyes, making sure to keep the eyelids and tear ducts intact and on the skin.

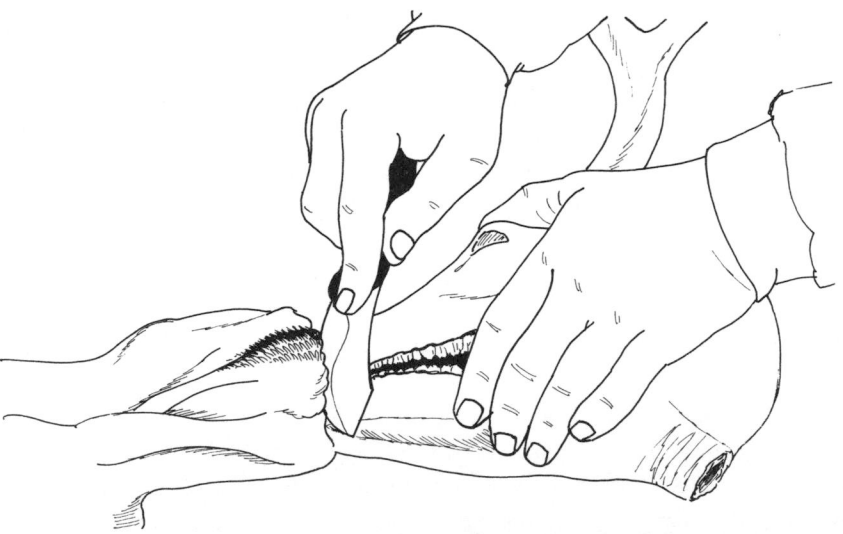

Cut the skin away from the sides of the jaw being careful not to cut the lip skin.

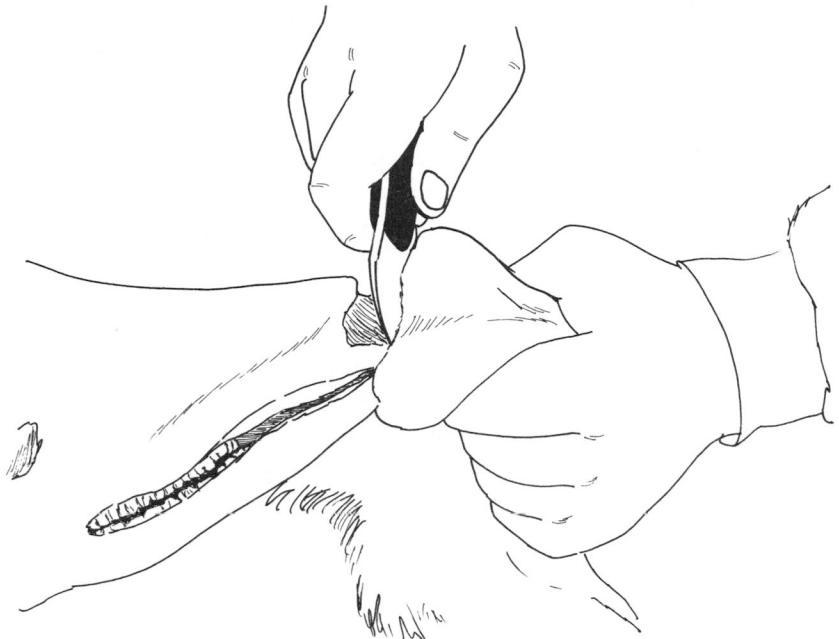

Continue carefully cutting the skin away from the nose and mouth area until the cape is free.

Starting on the bridge of the nose, continue skinning down the muzzle to the nostrils. Peel the skin back from the bone, and carefully cut through the nose cartilage to the bone. You can insert your fingers into the nostrils to guide this, but make sure you don't cut your fingers in the process. Continue, carefully cutting until the nose and upper lip are free.

If you're going to freeze the cape or get it to a taxidermist fairly quickly, apply salt to all exposed surfaces.

FLESHING THE CAPE

If, however, you still have some time before getting the cape to the taxidermist or a freezer, you should flesh the cape, skin out the ears, and remove as much cartilage and flesh from the cape as possible.

To skin out the ears, fold them wrong side out, and cut carefully between the outside covering and the cartilage. The cartilage is firmly attached to the front of the ear but not the back. Once the ear has been about half skinned, use a butter knife, a flat pointed stick, or wide flat screwdriver to work between the skin on the back and the cartilage in the front of the ear. Continue working until you can turn the ear inside out. Remove all muscle from the ear butt, leaving the cartilage attached to the front ear skin. Apply plenty of salt on both the cartilage and the ear skin, then turn the ear back right side out.

The lips consist of muscle with skin on both sides. They must be split open, leaving cheek skin and mouth skin, in order for the salt to reach all of the skin. Scrape all the flesh away from the skin inside the lips, but not deeply enough to loosen the whiskers. Also trim all flesh away from the nostrils.

Continue to remove all flesh from the cape.

SALTING THE CAPE

After the cape is fleshed, lay it flat. Apply salt, spreading it evenly over the entire fleshed surface of the cape, paying special attention to the eyes, lips, and ears. Make sure the cape has no folds or creases that prevent salt from contacting the skin.

Noniodized salt is the best, and it requires approximately 2 pounds for a whitetail deer cape and upwards of 4 pounds for elk or caribou. Once the cape is thoroughly salted, fold it lengthwise, and place it in a safe location that is cool and shady and away from the direct sunlight. Allow the cape to drain for approximately 24 hours.

After allowing the cape to drain, open it up and examine it carefully to make sure the salt has penetrated all portions of the skin. If not, add more salt. If it is well covered, open the cape and allow it to dry, but still keep it in a cool, shady place. Do not expose the cape to direct sunlight or heat. When the cape begins to stiffen, fold it into a loose bundle, flesh side out for shipping or storage.

SKULL CAP AND ANTLERS

Once the cape has been removed, the antlers and skull cap can be removed by sawing through the skull at the crown. Cut through the middle of the eye sockets toward the back of the skull and parallel

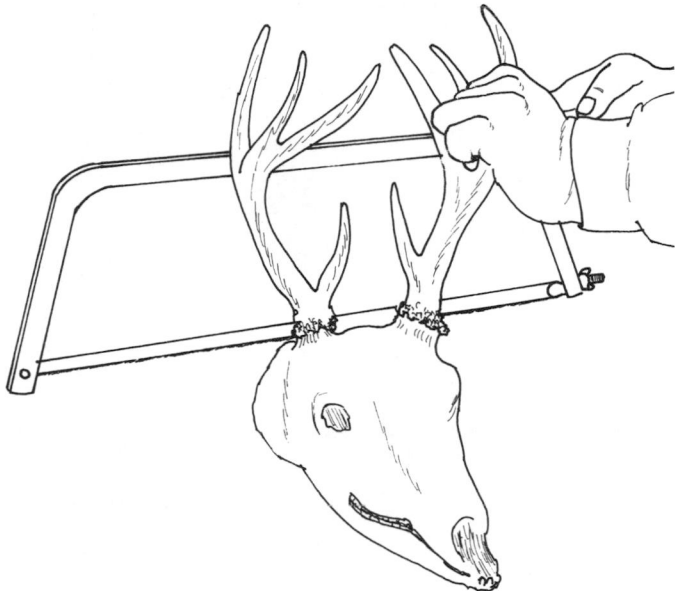

Then cut the antlers and skull plate away from the skull.

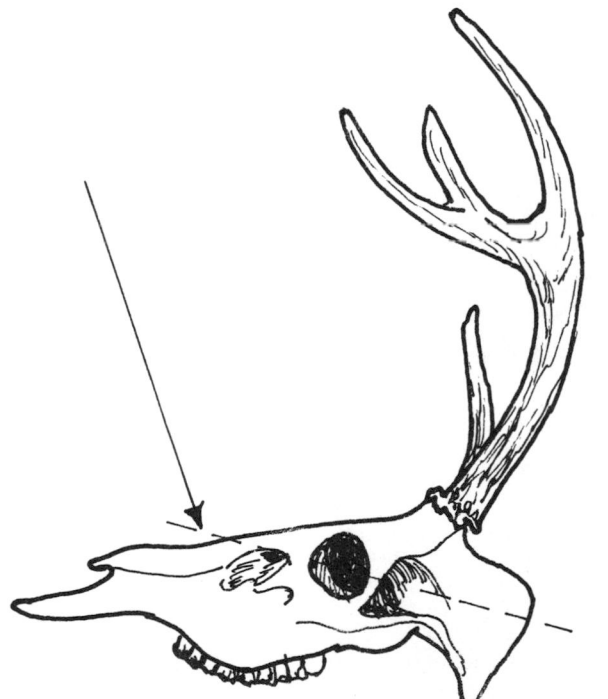

The cut to release the antlers should be made along the line shown.

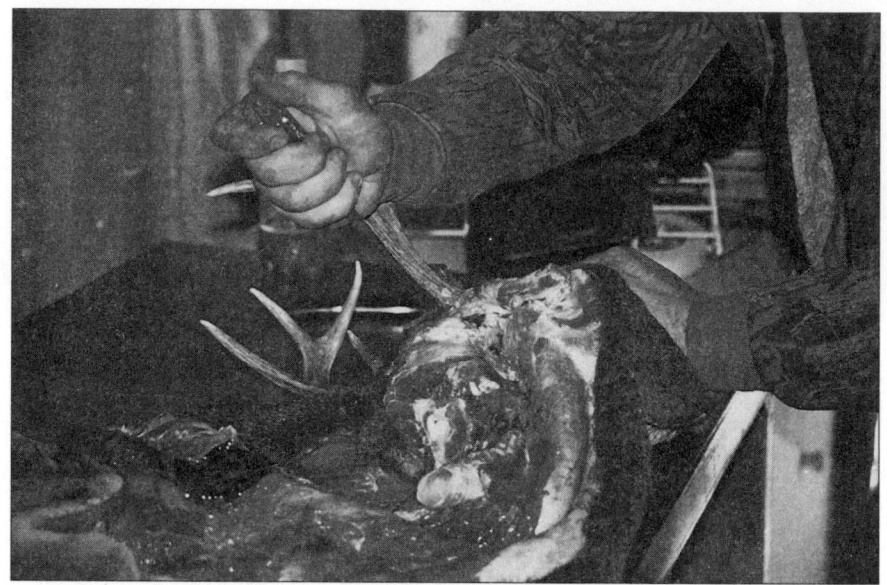

Caping is a fairly easy job if you take your time and pay attention.

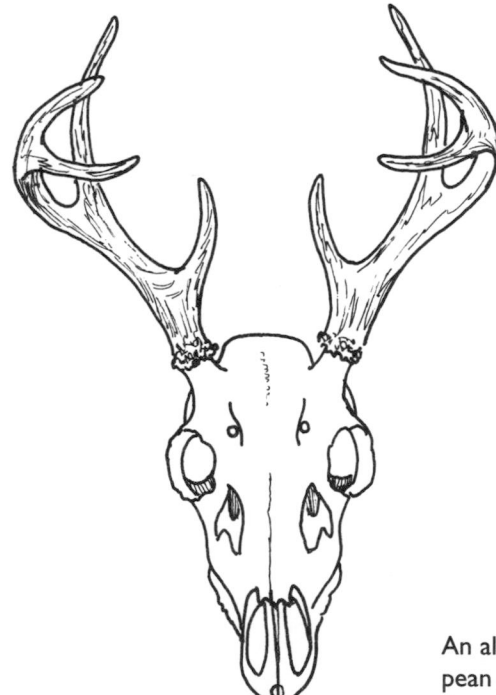

An alternative to a full mount is a European mount and these are quite easily done at home.

to the bottom of the lower jaw. Remove the brains from the skull pan and any attached meat, then salt the inside and outside thoroughly.

In some instances, only the skull plate is used, mounting it directly to a plaque or board and covering it with felt or other materials.

EUROPEAN MOUNT

An alternative to a full head mount is a European mount. These can easily be done at home, providing a beautiful mount without the cost of a full taxidermy mount. They also take up less space than a full head mount. In this case, the skull is skinned completely, then bleached to a pure white and mounted on a board or plaque.

The first step is to remove the head from the spinal column, then skin out the head in the same manner as described for caping for a full skin mount. You don't, of course, have to be as precise around the eyes, ears, and nose. It is important in this case, however, to make sure you don't slice or cut into the skull during the skinning process.

Once the cape is skinned out, remove the eyes, detach the lower jaw by cutting through the muscle at each side, and then cut away the tongue.

Place the head in a large pot on an outdoor stove, such as a Coleman camp stove, and boil for several hours to soften the tissue on the skull. The skull should be covered with water up to—but must be below—the antler bases. A handful of washing soda should be used to help cut the grease. The biggest problem is finding a pot big enough for this chore; afterward, it's fairly hard to clean the pot. You don't want to do this chore inside. The water should be at a rolling boil before you place the head in it. Place the head in the water, and turn down the heat immediately to simmer the solution. As the water level drops, add hot water to maintain the correct level.

After a couple of hours, remove the skull, allow it to cool, and pull off and cut away the flesh, muscles, and membranes. As you pour off the solution, check for any teeth or loose pieces of bone that may have fallen off.

Place the head back in the pot, add fresh water and more washing soda, and simmer again for another hour or so. Again, make sure the water is at a full rolling boil before adding the skull, then immediately lower the heat to simmer. Remove the skull, allow it to cool, and then continue to remove any flesh or membrane.

The hardest part is removing the brains from inside the skull. A piece of stiff wire or coat-hanger wire can be used to break up the tissue that remains after simmering and allow the tissue to be pulled out through the brain stem opening in the bottom of the skull. Flush with hot water several times to assure all brain matter has been removed.

The skull must be whitened to produce the beautiful stark white appearance. Use 40 percent hydrogen peroxide and hairdressers' whitener, both found at your local beauty shop or beauty supply store, or 40 percent hydrogen peroxide and dry-powdered bleach. Do not use drugstore hydrogen peroxide as it is too weak, and do not use laundry bleach as it tends to soften the bones. Mix the two in a nonmetallic bowl, then, wearing rubber gloves and goggles, apply the mixture to the skull. Place the coated skull in a clear plastic bag and place it in the direct sunlight on a white surface. Leave it for a couple of days, then wash off the bleaching solution with a mild vinegar solution and rinse the skull in clean water.

CHAPTER 5

Butchering

C utting up a carcass, especially a large animal such as a big deer, can seem quite daunting to the beginner. Many years ago, when I made my first attempt, my wife Joan issued a simple, reassuring statement. "Doesn't matter how it's done, it all goes into the pot." She was right. Since that time, I've learned any number of tactics can be used to cut up a carcass, and all with good results. The key is to have all your equipment ready and a good place to work as described in Chapter 1, then to simply take your time and enjoy it. Cutting up meat can be a pleasant after-the-hunt chore. In fact, growing up in the old days, butchering day was a social affair. Neighbors came for miles to bring fat hogs to slaughter and to work together, often butchering upwards of a dozen animals. My family has extended this fun social event with a weekend of butchering following a successful deer season.

Two methods can be used for cutting up the carcass. The method depends on the meat cuts you prefer, the age and size of the animal, how many people you intend to feed, your preferences in meat cuts, and your equipment. You can use a saw for the initial cuts and cut the carcass in the traditional manner (the same as used for beef with the larger animals and the same as used for lamb or goat for smaller deer or antelope size). This method provides the more tender cuts for steaks, medium tender cuts that must be tenderized, and the tougher cuts to be ground into hamburger. Shown is a chart illustrating the typical cuts from the various parts of the carcass and how they are used. You can use a handsaw to slice the various roasts and steaks, but it's a lot of work. A powered meat saw is best for the chore. If you can find a used one, it's a good investment if you intend to do much butchering.

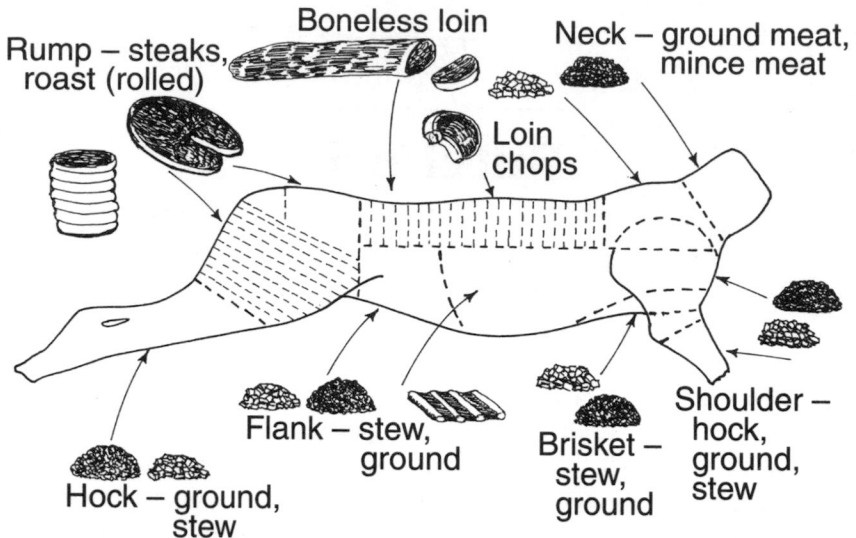

Shown are the standard butcher cuts and the resulting meat from the various portions of the carcass.

If you don't have a powered meat saw, you can simply cut all the meat away from the bone. The bone-in method provides traditional cuts but is much harder to do. The boneless is the easiest to do, requires less equipment, and takes up much less freezer space. Many of the same cuts can be used in the same manner, only without the hassle of the bone. In the boneless method, especially on small deer, the ribs are quite often not used.

Over the years, I've discovered that a combination of the two methods can also be used.

The traditional method is to first split the carcass in half. This provides the traditional "chops" with the backbone in. In cool weather, and if you have a protected place to hang the carcass, you may wish to skin out the animal, then split the carcass in half for the hanging process. This allows for more rapid cooling of the meat. Leave a connecting piece of meat on the neck to keep the carcass halves intact for easier handling until you're ready for butchering.

To cut the carcass in half, suspend it by the hocks and use a hand meat saw to split down the centerline of the backbone, starting at the point where the tail was removed. Slicing down through the muscle with a knife will help reveal the centerline of the bone.

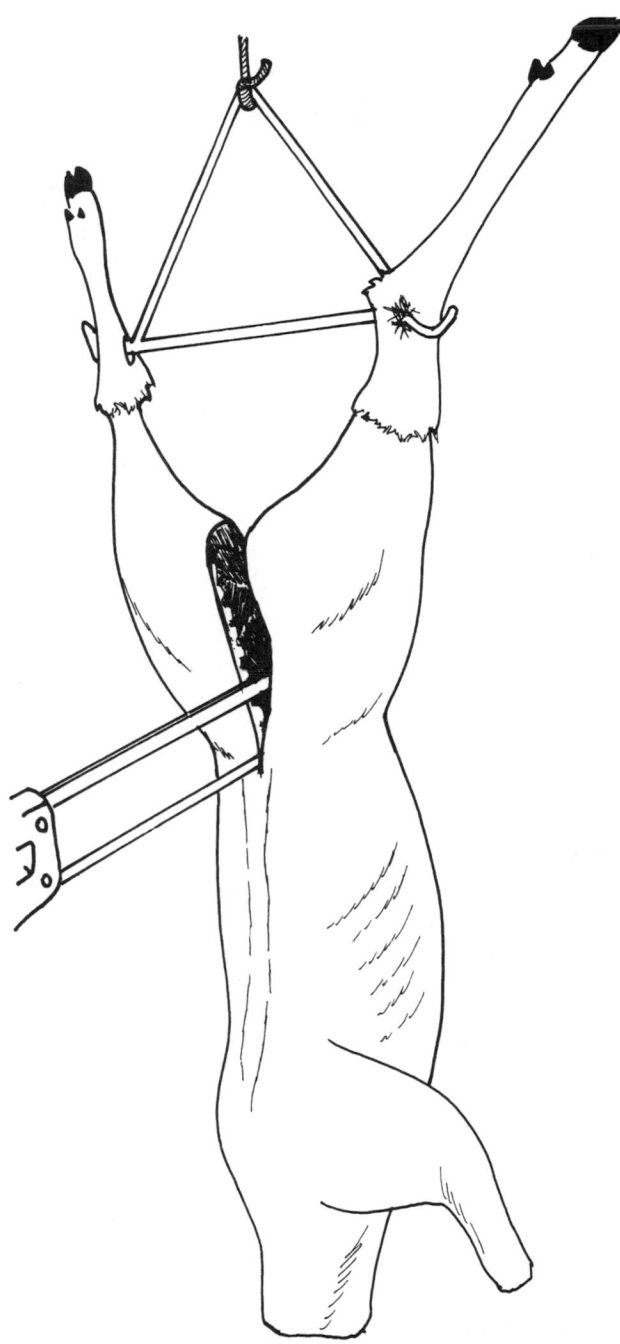

Deer carcasses can be halved, and cut up in the same traditional manner as beef to produce backbone-in chops.

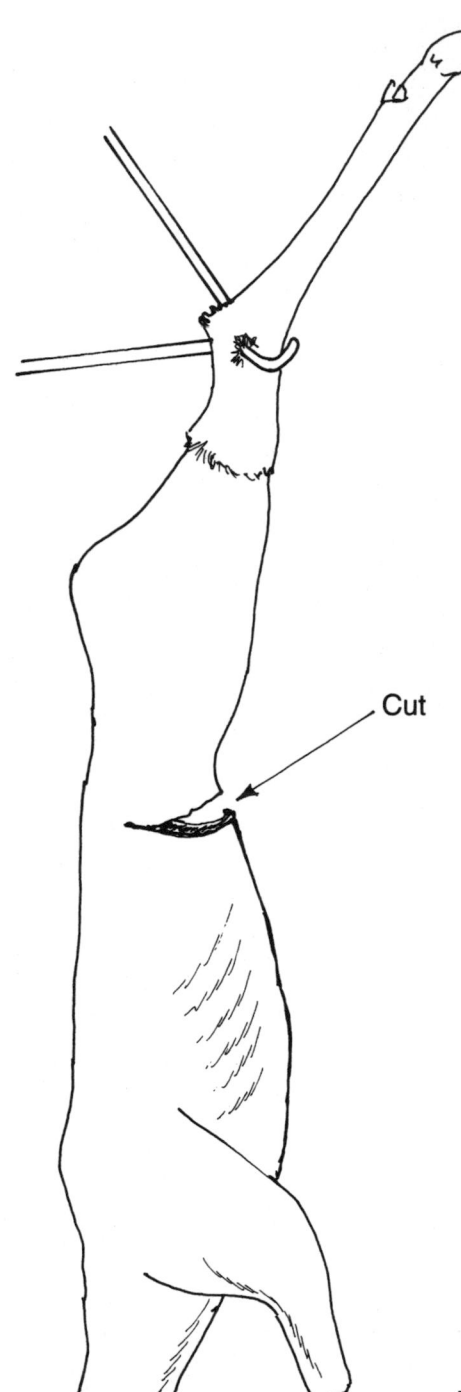

Cut

The halves are then quartered.

Saw straight down the center of the neck bone and through the neck to complete the cut.

If you have a larger carcass to cut, the handsaw can be used, but it becomes a chore. A chain saw can make shorter work of it, but the blade and chain must be clean. I keep an electric chain saw on hand just for this purpose.

Once the carcass has been split in half, the next step is to quarter it. On large animals, this is best done while the carcass is hanging. Smaller animals can be laid flat on a work surface for quartering. On larger hanging carcasses, the traditional method is to make a cut between the last two ribs to the backbone. Begin this cut about 2 inches in from the front or flank, leaving a strip of meat intact in that location. Then saw the backbone to separate the quarters, leaving the strip of flank meat on the last rib to hold the quarter in place. One person can then grasp the quarter while another cuts the strip to separate the quarters. On smaller animals, one person can handle the quartering. Simply saw through the backbone, then cut through the flank below the last rib while holding the quarter.

FRONT QUARTER

Lay the front quarter on the cutting table with the skin side out. Starting about halfway down the exposed rib, make a cut across the carcass and across the shank. Use a knife to mark the cut, then a meat saw to complete cutting through the bone. This removes the

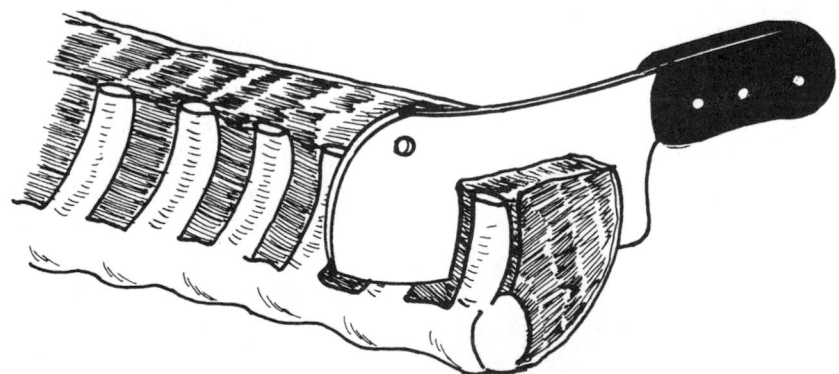

In this case the ribs are cut away from the backbone, leaving a short section and the backbone and backstraps cut into "chops."

brisket, plate, and foreshank. The foreshank can be cut crosswise into soup bones, and the upper portion of the shank can be cut into arm roasts. The rib section can be sawed into short ribs, cutting across the ribs, and the brisket removed. All of these cuts can also be trimmed into the ground meat if you prefer.

The neck is removed by cutting crosswise at the juncture of the shoulder. The neck meat is then most often boned out. It can be used as a rolled neck roast or boneless neck; in most cases, it is ground. Boning the neck is fairly easy, but it's important to cut away all the yellow cartilage surrounding the windpipe. Incidentally, we've discovered ground neck meat makes excellent mincemeat and that the neck from an average deer is just about the right amount to work up.

The upper portion of the shoulder is divided just behind the withers to create the chuck and the rib section. This is done with a hand meat saw to produce the two sections. The chuck or shoulder is then cut into roasts producing chuck roasts, cross arm roasts, or round bone chuck roasts, using either the hand meat saw or a powered meat band saw. Short ribs are cut from the lower part of the rib section, and the upper section is cut into standing rib, rolled (boneless) rib, or rib steaks.

Collect all trimmings from making the various cuts separately for grinding into venison burger.

HINDQUARTER

The next step is to cut up the hindquarter. Lay the quarter down on the table with the skin side down. Remove the flank—the triangular-shaped piece of meat on the lower front portion. The flank contains the flank steak, which can be pulled out. The rest of the flank, as well as the flank steak piece, can be used in hamburger.

Cut away the kidney and kidney fat from the backbone.

The hindquarter is then divided into four sections. Start by first dividing into two sections, the loin and round. Separate these two sections at the ball and socket hip joint. Start the cut with a knife, and complete it with the handsaw. The loin is then divided into a short loin and loin end, making the cut at the hip joint. The loin section produces the most popular steaks. The short loin produces the club, T-bone, and porterhouse steaks, and the loin end produces sirloin steaks. In the case of deer, these are also sometimes called "loin chops."

The round section is divided into two: the round and the rump. The rump is cut away from the round across the top of the section by sawing across the bone as shown. The rump makes a rump roast or a boneless rolled rump roast. The hind shank is cut away from the round, leaving a section that is cut into round steaks. Meat from the hind shank is used in burger, and the lower shank leg, or hock, is used as soup bones.

CUTTING SMALL DEER CARCASSES

Small deer can be cut in the same manner as lamb. With small carcasses, the entire carcass is handled as one piece rather than in quarters. The carcass is usually not split, but in hot weather the carcass may need to be split to cool quickly.

The first cut is made by sawing off the front shoulder between the fifth and sixth ribs. Once the shoulder has been removed, the neck is cut off flush with the front of the shoulder. The left and right shoulders are then separated by sawing down the backbone, creating two small roasts. These can be left bone in, or the bone can be removed, creating a rolled roast.

The shank, flank, breast, and neck are all boned and ground into burger or diced into stew meat.

The breast piece is removed by cutting forward across the flank with a saw with the carcass on its side. The rack portion is then cut from the loin between the two last ribs. The rack can be made into a standing crown roast or can be split into chops. The first step is to separate into two pieces a left and right side.

To create a standing crown roast, lay the crown section on its back and saw the ribs from each side of the backbone, but leave the meat attached. Then, using a boning saw, trim out the backbone, leaving the ribs attached without separating the two rib sections. Remove about an inch or so of meat between the ribs on their outer ends. The last step is to bend the sections into a round shape and tie the two sets together with string.

The loin is removed from the leg at the small of the back- or pinbone. Begin the cut with a knife and complete it with a saw down through the backbone.

The technique of cutting and preparing a leg of lamb can also be used on very small hoofed game as well. After removing the loin, the legs are separated by splitting them down through the center of the backbone with a saw.

Leg of "deer" can be prepared American or French style and will bring out the connoisseurs. In American style, the majority of the shank bone is removed, allowing it to fit in a smaller pan. The shank is removed approximately 2 inches from the shank joint.

BONING

Boning out the meat is relatively simple, and you really can't make serious mistakes. If boning an animal, I leave the carcass hanging for the initial steps, simply cutting sections away so I don't have to lift or handle as large a piece at one time.

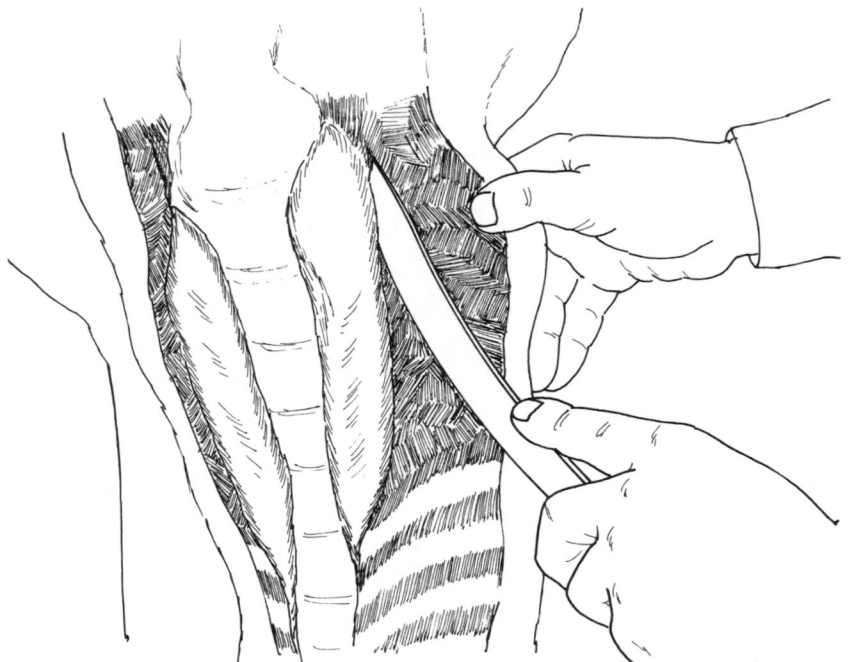

An easier method is to "quarter" and partially "bone out" the carcass while it hangs. The first step is to remove the tenderloins located inside the body, next to the backbone.

The first step is to remove the tenderloins from inside the rib cage. These will easily pull out after the carcass has cooled. A little judicious cutting with a sharp boning knife will help to get them started. These are the most tender parts of the animal and make great little steaks, either grilled or lightly fried.

The next step is to remove the front shoulder. It comes off quite easily without any sawing. Slice directly between the shoulder and the side, starting at the lower junction between the leg and the brisket and slicing toward the top or back of the animal. Lift up the leg as you slice, and it will come off easily. A deer shoulder usually doesn't have a lot of meat, and in many cases, one or more of the shoulders may be damaged from the shot. All of the muscles in the shoulder and front shank are long, filled with sinew, and fairly tough. In my opinion, they are best used in ground meat and stew meat or sliced into jerky. The shoulder can be boned quite easily by simply slicing long sections, going with the grain of the meat, into the small chunks used for grinding.

The next step is to remove the backstrap. With the carcass still hanging, slide the blade of the boning knife along both sides of the backbone down and to the ribs, from the juncture of the top of the hips to the neck. Turn the knife and follow the angle of the ribs to make a second cut to release the backstrap on one side. Once you get the backstrap started, it will usually peel out fairly easily, only requiring further cutting at the ends to release it. Repeat on the opposite backstrap.

With both shoulders and the backstraps removed from the hanging carcass, cut across the carcass just above the ribs with a knife, then have someone hold the front half while another person saws through the backbone. This produces a front rib section that's fairly manageable. Lay the rib section on a table, and proceed to bone out the neck as described earlier.

Cut away all of the outer rib meat, undershoulder meat, the brisket, and any other scraps that remain. All of these can go into the ground-meat pot. You can also use a small boning knife to remove the pieces between the ribs, or simply boil the ribs to remove the meat for use in a soup base.

You can bone out the rear section all in one piece, especially on smaller deer. I prefer, however, to cut the rear section into two sections for easier handling. This is done by sawing down the back-

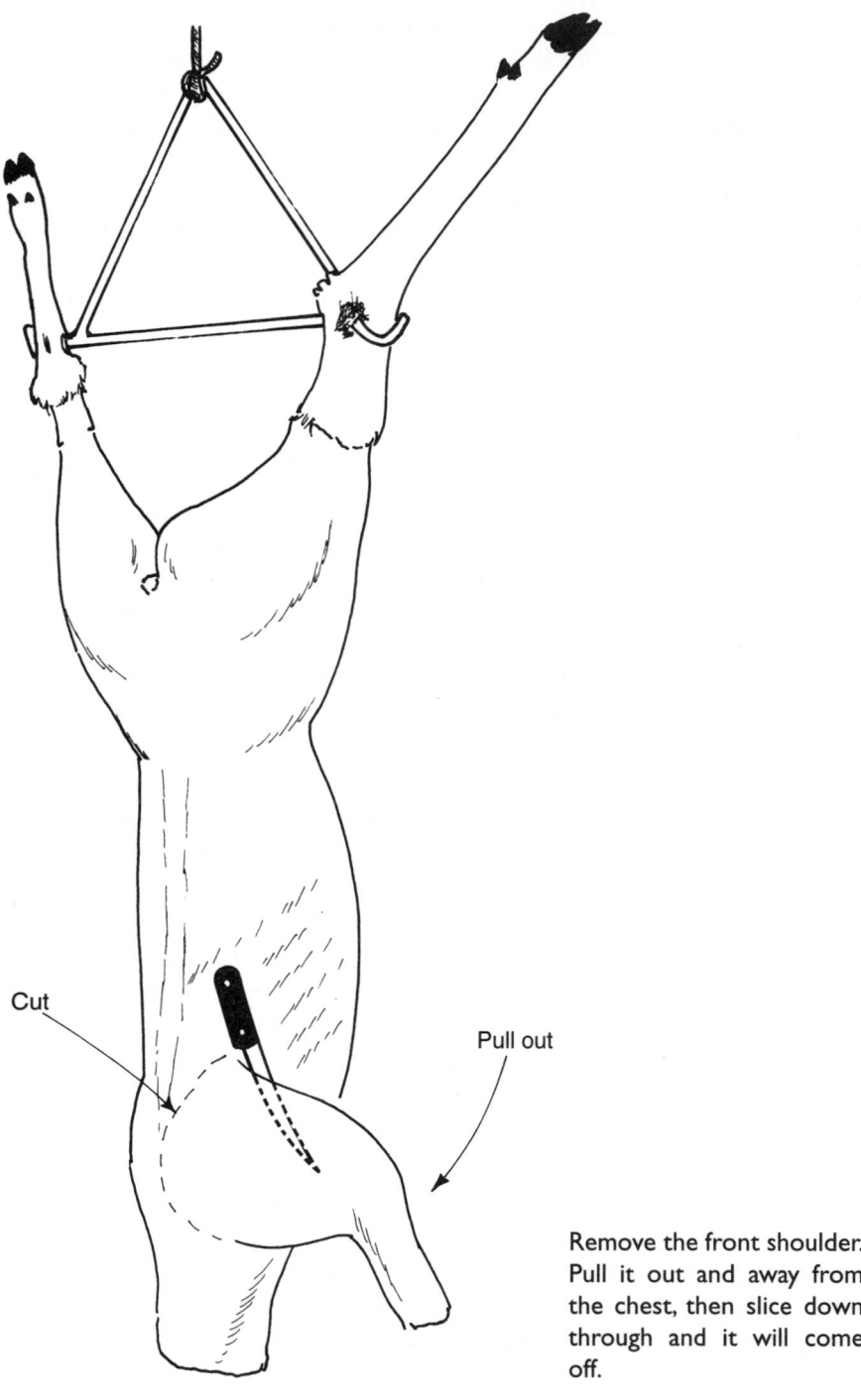

Cut

Pull out

Remove the front shoulder. Pull it out and away from the chest, then slice down through and it will come off.

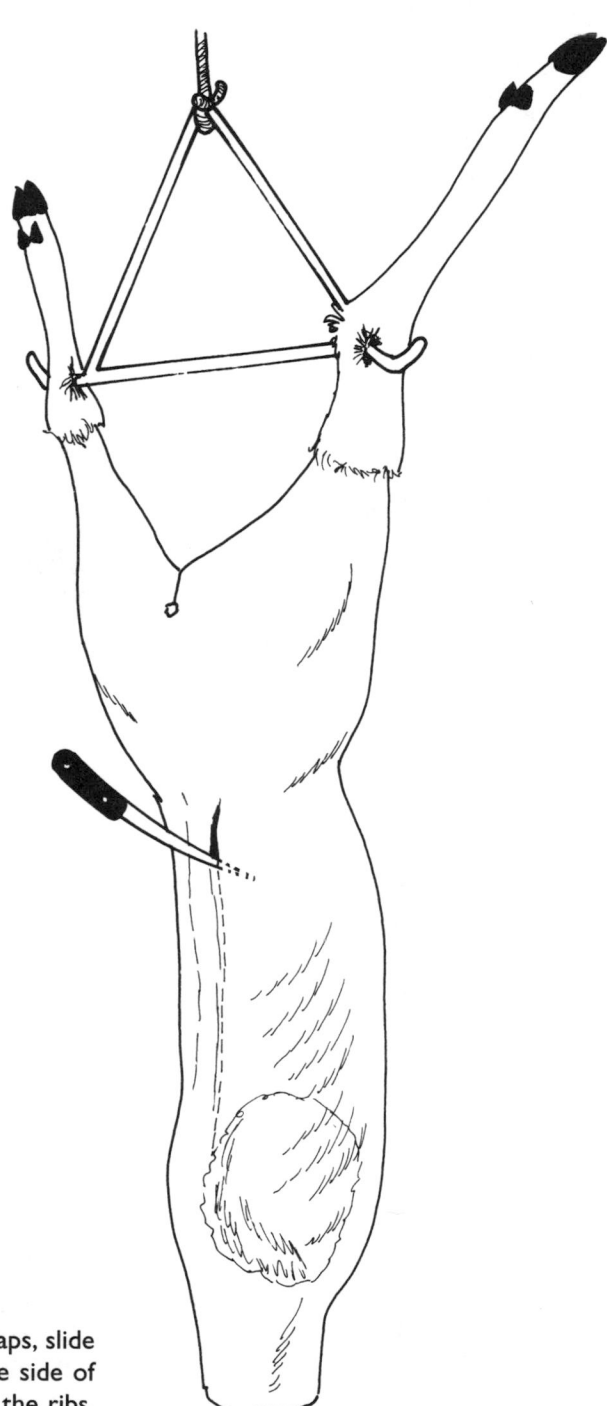

To remove the backstraps, slide
a boning knife along the side of
the backbone down to the ribs.

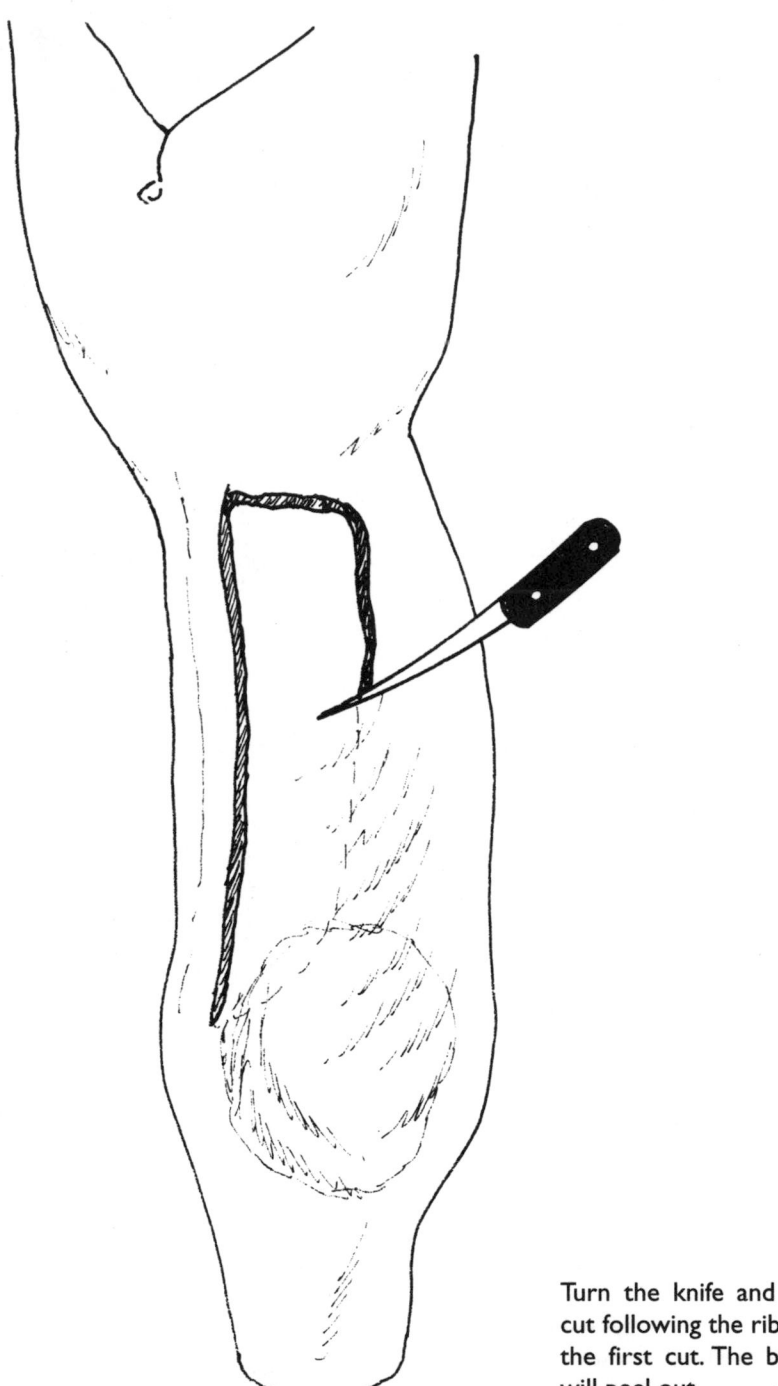

Turn the knife and make a cut following the ribs to join the first cut. The backstrap will peel out.

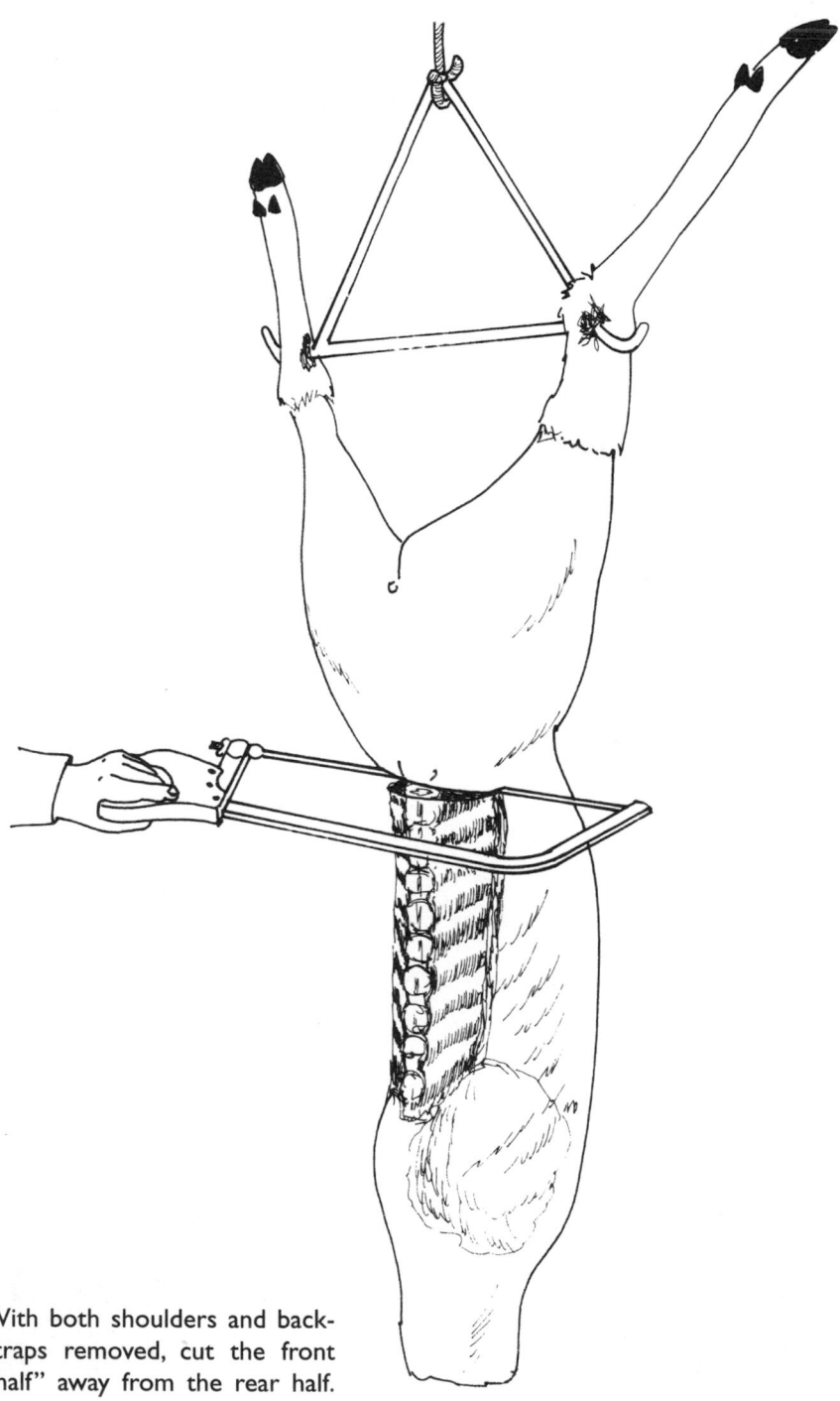

With both shoulders and back-straps removed, cut the front "half" away from the rear half.

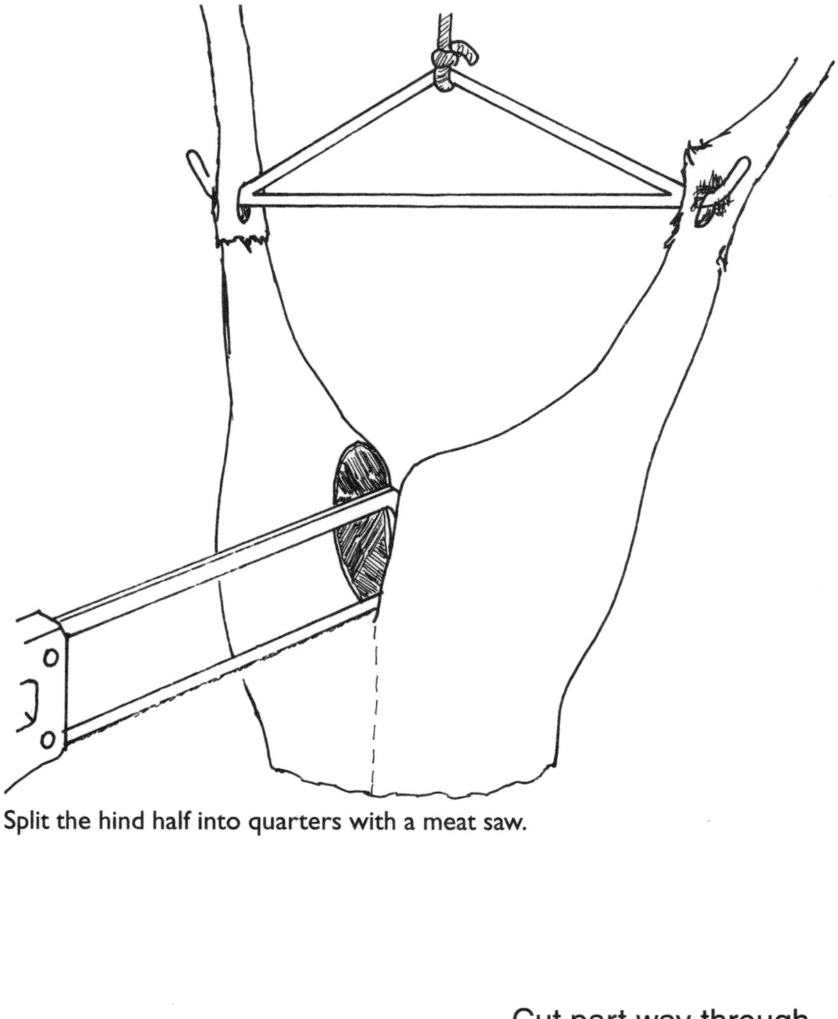

Split the hind half into quarters with a meat saw.

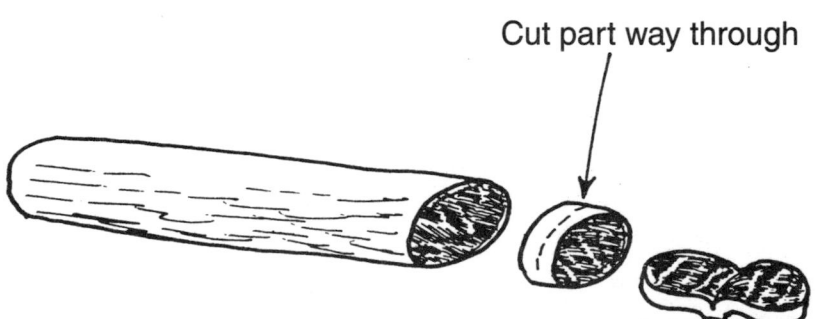

Cut part way through

The backstrap is sliced and can be butterfly cut to produce bigger pieces.

bone with a handsaw. It doesn't require much effort to saw the short distance to separate the pieces.

The ham is "muscled" out, or cut into sections following the muscles. You can remove the ham in one piece fairly easily, but I prefer to cut it into two main sections, which are used for round

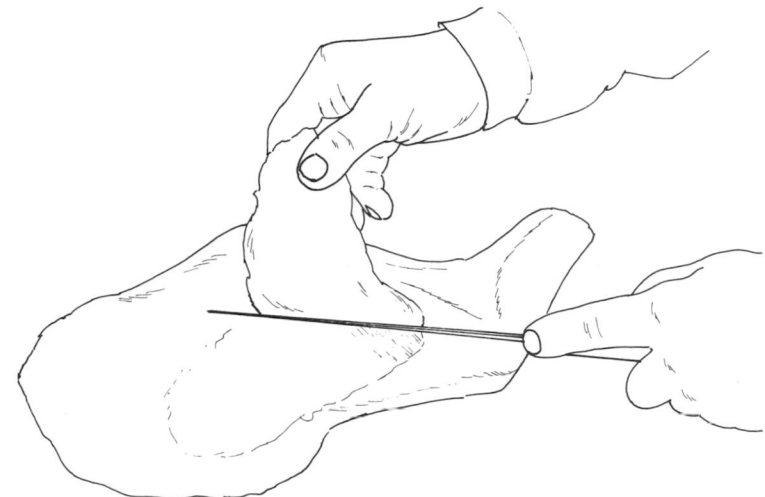

Bone out the ribs, neck, and shoulders.

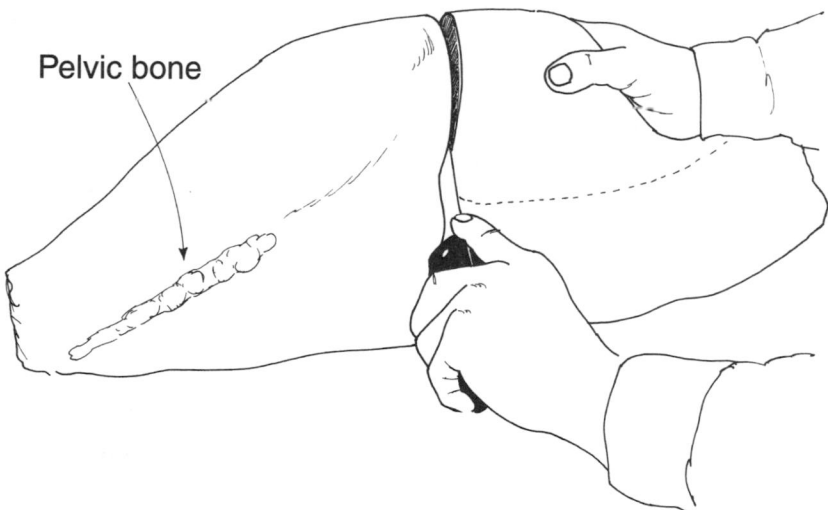

Pelvic bone

You can make a roast or steaks from the ham by boning it out.

steaks or roasts. Trim the remainder of the ham into scraps for either soup, stew meat, or ground meat. The shank is trimmed out in the same manner as for the foreshank. The hindquarter bones can also be separated at the joint and boiled to remove the rest of the meat and produce a soup stock.

Once all the cuts have been made, it's important to remove all fat from between the muscles. Cut away any gristle as well.

All trimmings, as well as designated ground-meat pieces, should be collected in a clean container as the carcass is cut up. These should be ground as soon as possible. The longer the meat sits, the more blood collects. If you can't immediately grind it, place it in a refrigerator until you can.

GROUND MEAT

Wild game can be ground and used by itself, ground with other meats, or other ground meats can be added. We actually prefer deer meat ground by itself. The reason is that we take a great deal of care in preparing the meat to be ground. We also prefer the meat without fat added except when making meat patties for grilling or frying. Then we purchase inexpensive "fatty" hamburger and mix pound for pound with ground venison from the freezer to make patties suitable for grilling or frying. Some like to add a pound of

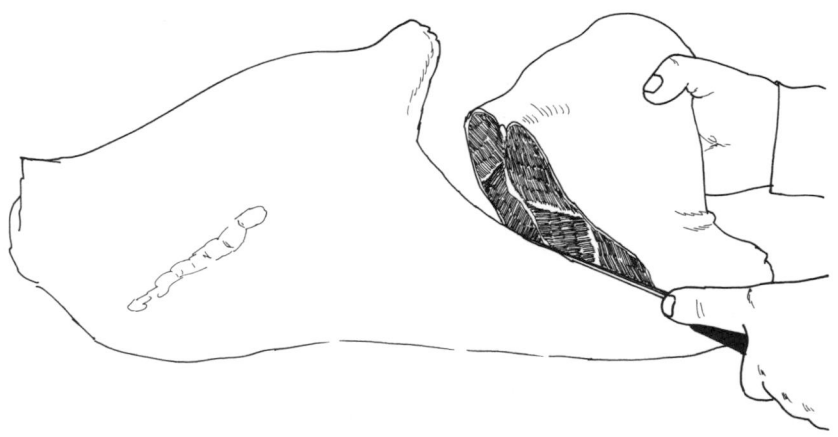

Use a boning knife and follow the bones.

beef fat into the lean venison from a deer when grinding, but that makes all the ground meat fat.

The key to good ground venison is to remove all fat from in and around the tissues. As much sinew as possible must also be removed, as it makes grinding tough with a power grinder and almost impossible with a hand grinder. The meat to be ground should be cut into 2-inch chunks to further facilitate grinding as well as expose fat and tissues that must be removed.

SAFETY CONCERNS

Make sure you keep the butchering area clean. Wash knives as needed between cutting processes. Clean all grinding and stuffing equipment with a mixture containing 1 tablespoon of chlorine laundry bleach per 1 gallon of water. Clean all hair away from the meat.

6

Preserving Venison

Venison can be preserved by a number of methods, including freezing, canning, corning, made into sausage or jerky, and dried or smoked. Back in the old days, before freezing and canning, venison was made into a smoke dried jerky. In fact, techniques for making jerky are evident from many of the earliest cultures including the Egyptians.

JERKY

Jerky is still a great way of preserving the meat and provides a tasty, healthy snack food. One of my favorite pastimes is to sit in a deer stand waiting for a deer to come by, all the while chewing on a piece of jerky from the previous season. Jerky is actually removing moisture from the food, thereby preventing enzymes from contacting or reacting with the meat. In the past, jerky making consisted of soaking the meat in a marinade, then simply drying it in an oven or dehydrator. Most dehydrators achieve a temperature of 140 degrees F. Recent outbreaks of illnesses caused by *Salmonella* and *Escherichia coli* (*E. coli*) from eating homemade jerky have raised some safety concerns in regards to the traditional methods used.

According to the United States Department of Agriculture (USDA) Food Safety and Inspection Service (FSIS), "When raw meat or poultry is dehydrated at home—either in a warm oven or a food dehydrator—to make jerky which will be stored on the shelf, pathogenic bacteria are likely to survive the dry heat of a warm oven and especially the 130 to 140°F of a food dehydrator." Following is their recommended methods of properly drying jerky:

The trimmings from boning and other portions of venison are best ground using a meat grinder.

Due to the possibility of illness from *Salmonella* and *E. coli* 0157:H7 from homemade jerky, the USDA current recommendation for making jerky safely is to heat meat to 160°F before the dehydrating process. This step assures that any bacteria present will be destroyed by wet heat. But most dehydrator instructions do not include this step, and a dehydrator may not reach temperatures high enough to heat meat to 160°F. After heating to 160°F, maintaining a constant dehydrator temperature of 130 to 140°F during the drying process is important because (1) the process must be fast enough to dry food before it spoils; and (2) it must remove enough water that microorganisms are unable to grow.

The USDA recommends the following safe handling and preparation methods:

- Always wash hands thoroughly with soap and water before and after working with meat products.
- Use clean equipment and utensils.

- Keep meat and poultry refrigerated at 40°F or slightly below; use or freeze ground meats and poultry within 2 days; whole red meats, within 3 to 5 days.
- Defrost frozen meat in the refrigerator, not on the kitchen counter.
- Marinate meat in the refrigerator. Don't save marinade to re-use. Marinades are used to tenderize and flavor the jerky before dehydrating it.
- Steam or roast meat and poultry to 160°F as measured with a meat thermometer before dehydrating it.
- Dry meats in a food dehydrator that has an adjustable temperature dial and will maintain a temperature of at least 130 to 140°F throughout the drying process.

Following is a quite simple method for making jerky. I like to partially freeze the meat to make slicing easier. An electric slicer can also make the chore easier. Trim away all fat (which can create off flavors), and as much connective tissue as possible from the meat. Then cut the meat into strips about ¼-inch thick with the grain, rather than across the grain. Combine the meat with Lawry's Seasoned Marinade or other bottled or packaged marinade in a glass bowl or zippered plastic bag and refrigerate for at least 2 hours.

Or use the following ingredients to make your own marinade:

1 tablespoon garlic salt
1 tablespoon lemon pepper
1 tablespoon onion powder
Tabasco Sauce (from a few drops to one or more tablespoons depending on taste)
1 cup soy sauce
Water to cover

Again, combine marinade and meat in a glass bowl or zippered plastic bag and refrigerate 12 hours or overnight.

Remove the meat, shake excess marinade from the strips, pat dry, and sprinkle with seasoned salt and garlic pepper. For spicier jerky, use the seasoned salt plus seasoned pepper or Cajun seasoning.

The jerky can then be dried in the oven or dehydrator following the USDA temperature recommendations.

Oven Drying

Place a sheet of aluminum foil in the bottom of your stove's oven to catch any drippings and drape the meat over the oven racks, leaving enough space between pieces for the air to circulate. Spraying the oven racks with a cooking spray keeps the jerky strips from sticking. The oven should be set to 350 degrees F and the meat baked until the internal temperature reaches 160 degrees F. Then set the oven to 170 degrees F or higher, and prop the door open 2 to 6 inches.

Most jerky will take 5 or 6 hours to dry, but times vary, depending on the heat of your individual oven and the thickness of the meat. Check for doneness after 3 hours and remove pieces as they become dry. Jerky is done when you can still bend it—overdone when it snaps. Store the finished product in a cool, dry place. Vacuum sealing also works well for storing jerky.

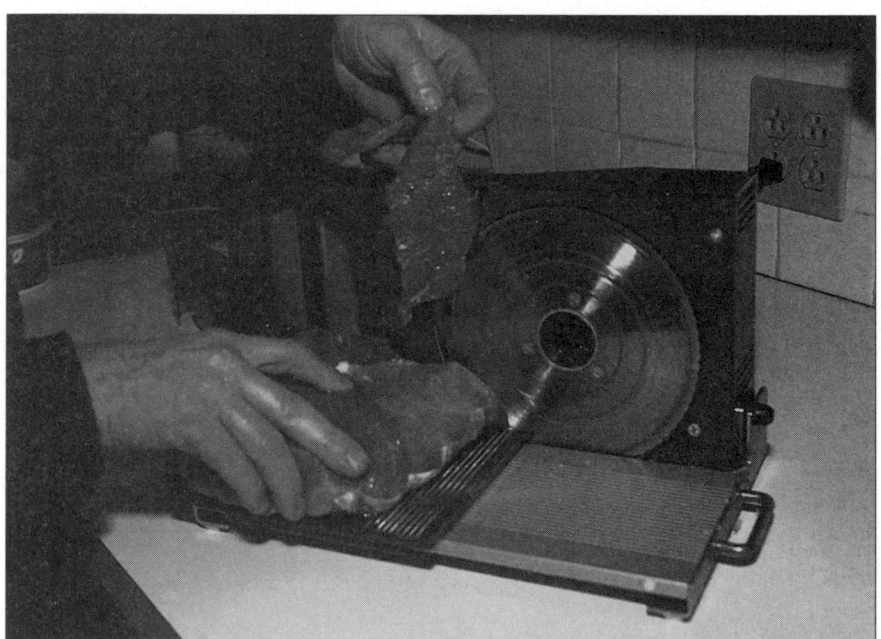

Jerky is one of the most popular ways of preserving venison. First step in making traditional jerky is to slice the meat thinly with the grain.

Marinade Cooked Jerky

Another method is simmering jerky in marinade before drying, as suggested by Penn State College of Agricultural Sciences:

Prepare 2–3 cups of your favorite marinade and bring it to a rolling boil over medium heat. Add a few meat strips, making sure the marinade covers them. Reheat to a full boil. (*Note:* It is not advised to presoak the strips in marinade. Putting unmarinated strips into boiling marinade minimizes any cooked flavors and maintains the safety of the marinade.) Remove the pan from the heat source. Remove the strips from the hot marinade and place them in a single, nonoverlapping layer on drying racks.

Dry the strips at 140 to 150 degrees F in a dehydrator, oven, or smoker.

Ground Jerky

Although jerky is traditionally made by slicing the meat into strips, it can also be made from ground meat using any number of jerky-making machines. This is actually a better way of using the tougher cuts of meat. Once ground and formed back into strips, the jerky is much easier to chew. Grinders and jerky-making machines are available from Cabela's and Bass Pro.

The first step is to grind the meat. Then place it in a plastic or stainless-steel bowl and add dry jerky flavoring. A number of mixes are available for this, or you can make your own, following this recipe:

5 pounds ground venison
5 heaping teaspoons Morton Tender Quick Salt or 1½ level
 teaspoons per pound of ground venison
¼ cup brown sugar
1 teaspoon garlic powder
1 teaspoon onion powder
¼ to ½ teaspoon ground red pepper or ½ teaspoon dried red
 pepper flakes

Mix the spices together, then sprinkle them over the ground meat. Use your hands to mix them together, sprinkling a little of the spice

Jerky can also be made of ground meat using a "jerky" gun or shooter, such as those from Cabela's. First step is to grind, then add spices and allow to marinate overnight.

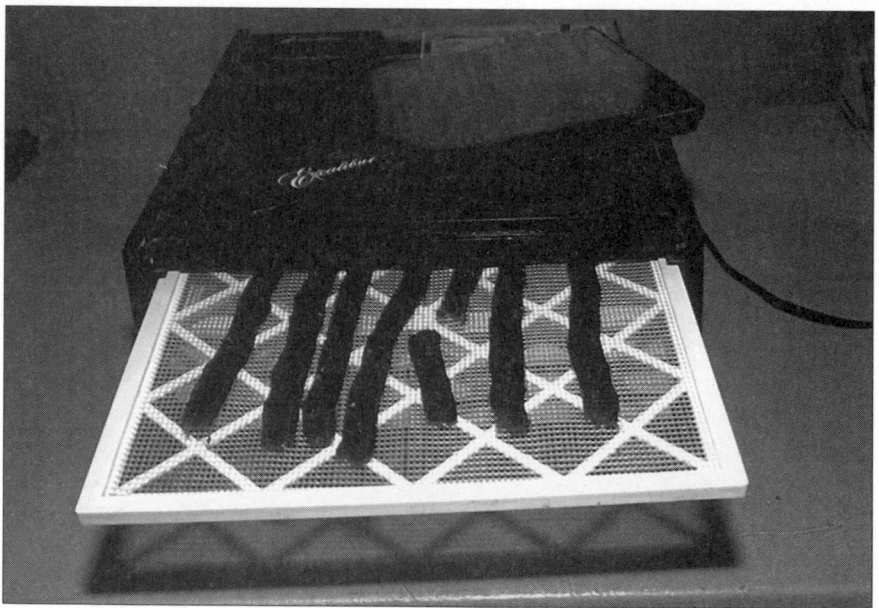

Jerky can be dried in an oven or dehydrator.

mixture, mixing that in, and adding more spices. Another mixing method is to dissolve the dry mixed spices in ¼ to ½ cup water. Stir until dissolved, then pour over the ground venison and mix in with hands or a large spoon. More or less of the garlic, onion, and red pepper can be added to suit. Always mix in an enameled, stainless-steel, or plastic container.

The meat is allowed to marinate with the mix in the refrigerator for 12 hours or overnight. Then place the ground and marinated meat in the jerky machine and extrude the meat into strips or sticks onto aluminum foil or a baking pan. Bake in the oven at 350 degrees F, until the interior temperature reaches 160 degrees F, then continue drying in the oven or dehydrator.

STORING JERKY

Jerky should be stored in clean plastic bags or jars, or wrapped in freezer paper and frozen. If not allowed to pick up moisture, jerky will keep indefinitely, but the quality and taste starts to deteriorate within a few months. Vacuum packing and freezing offer the best, long term storage method.

SAUSAGE

Next to jerky, sausage in one form or another is a very popular method of preserving deer meat. Sausages are made of ground meat. This is another method of using the tougher cuts. The most common sausages are the cooked/smoked varieties, and a number of different kinds can be made, depending on the spices and flavorings added. Flavorings and sausage stuffers are available from Luhr Jensen as well as the Sausage Maker and other companies listed in the back of the book. Following are the ingredients to make a variety of sausages. *Note:* For a less dry sausage, you can mix ground pork with the ground venison in proportions of one-fourth to one-half ground pork.

Meat is then extruded through a jerky gun and dried.

Pepperoni

For each pound of ground venison add the following:

1½ level teaspoons Morton Tender Quick or Morton Sugar Cure
½ teaspoon ground black pepper
½ teaspoon mustard seed
½ teaspoon fennel seed
½ teaspoon garlic powder
¼ teaspoon crushed red pepper flakes
¼ teaspoon anise seed

Combine ingredients and mix until well blended. Refrigerate 12 hours or overnight. Stuff sausages and smoke or bake until a meat thermometer inserted in the center reaches 160 degrees F.

Summer Sausage

For each pound of ground venison add the following:

1½ level teaspoons Morton Tender Quick or Morton Sugar Cure
½ teaspoon ground black pepper
½ teaspoon garlic powder
½ teaspoon whole mustard seed
⅛ teaspoon ground ginger
⅛ teaspoon ground coriander

Combine ingredients and mix until well blended. Refrigerate 12 hours or overnight. Stuff sausages and smoke or bake until a meat thermometer inserted in the center reaches 160 degrees F.

VENISON BOLOGNA

For each pound of ground venison add the following:

1½ level teaspoons Morton Tender Quick or Morton Sugar Cure
½ teaspoon ground black or white pepper
¼ teaspoon paprika
¼ teaspoon onion powder
⅛ teaspoon ground nutmeg
⅛ teaspoon allspice

Combine ingredients and mix until well blended. Refrigerate 12 hours or overnight. Stuff sausages and smoke or bake until a meat thermometer inserted in the center reaches 160 degrees F.

GRINDING SAUSAGE

The first step is to grind the meat. If using frozen meat, thaw in a refrigerator, not at room temperature. Keep the meat as cold as possible during the grinding and mixing processes. The meat should never be warmer than 40 degrees F. Make sure you use only good quality products including sodium nitrite (contained in the Morton Tender Quick meat cure). The sodium nitrite improves flavor, inhibits growth of *Clostridium botulinum* and gives the characteristic pink coloring.

If you have dual grinding plates, grind the meat first with a coarse grind plate then with a finer plate. Some recipes call for 75

Venison is quite often made into sausage. A dandy sausage making kit, complete with stuffer, casings, and spice cure is available from Luhr Jensen.

First step is to grind the meat.

percent of the meat to be ground with a coarse plate and 25 percent ground with a finer plate. Developing your own style is what venison sausage is all about. I would suggest keeping copious notes while sausage making until you develop a few favorites.

Then add the curing ingredients to the ground venison. It's a good idea to mix the ingredients in a bit of water to allow them to dissolve completely before adding to the sausage. Mix the curing ingredients thoroughly throughout the sausage. Allow the sausage and cure to set the required time as per the mix instructions in a refrigerator. Typically 12 hours or overnight.

STUFFING SAUSAGE

The sausage is then stuffed into casings. The casings may be hog casings, or synthetic casings. Hog casings must first be soaked in clean water before using and then rinsed completely. They're a bit more difficult to work with than synthetic casings. Synthetic casings must also be soaked, but do not need rinsing. Sausage casings are available from the Sausage Maker and others. The Luhr-Jensen kit comes complete with the casings needed.

Sausage may be stuffed in three ways: The Luhr Jensen Sausage Making Kit includes a variety of sausage mixes as well as a hand stuffer. The latter is a plastic tube over which the casings are fitted. The ground meat is then spooned into the stuffer and a hand-held plunger pushes the sausage through the tube into the casing.

The Sausage Maker has a tabletop mounted cast-iron stuffer that increases the volume of sausage that can be stuffed and reduces the time involved in stuffing casings. The unit is made to be fastened to a table or work surface. I fastened the stuffer to a board and the board can then be clamped to the tabletop with a wooden or c-clamp. This allows the unit to be removed for cleaning and storage when not in use.

Most of today's electric meat grinders also come with sausage stuffers. Some may allow the use of grinding plates so you can regrind with smaller openings as well. This is the quickest and easiest method of stuffing the sausages.

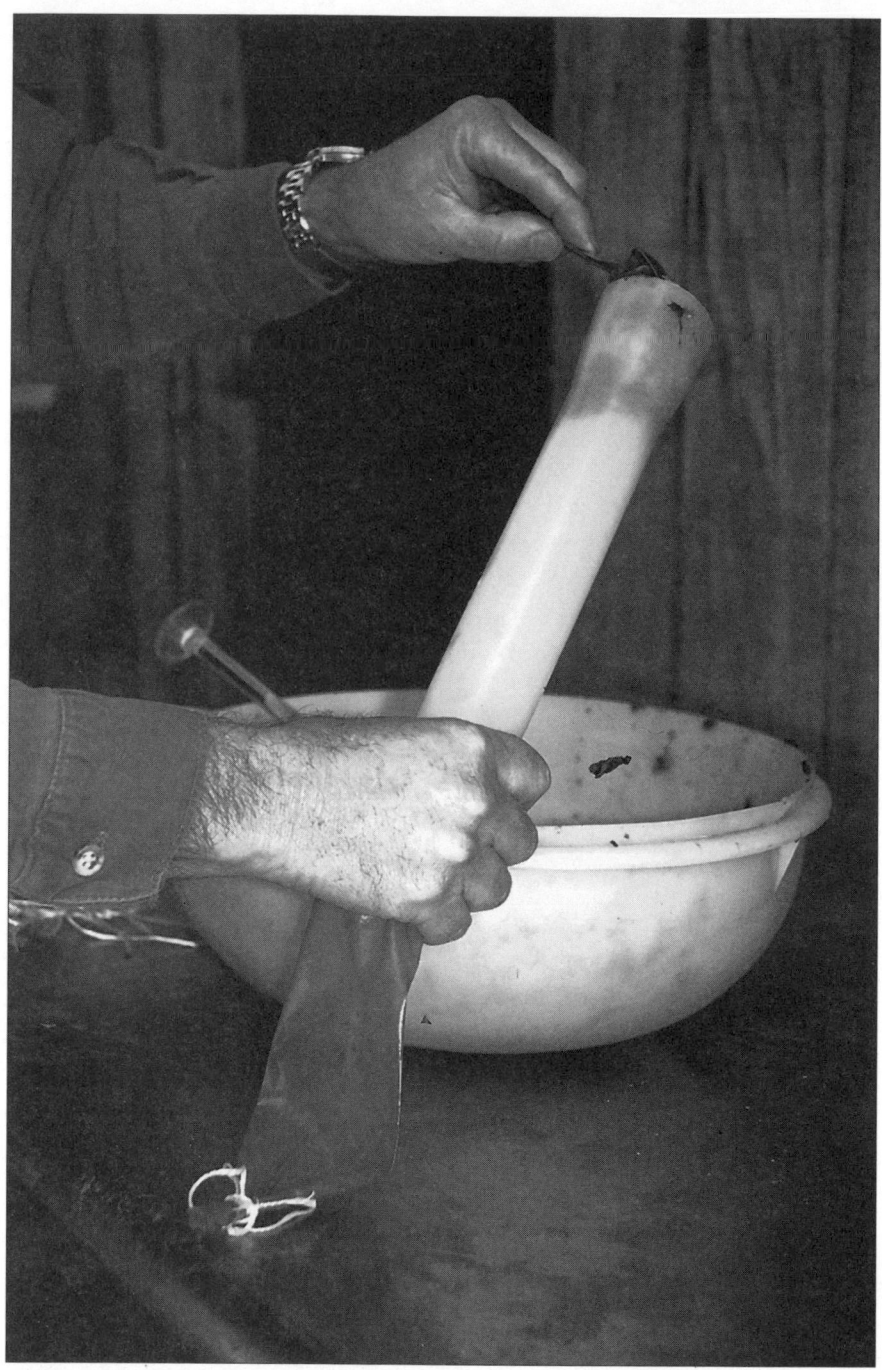

Then stuff in the casings. Shown is a Luhr-Jensen sausage stuffer.

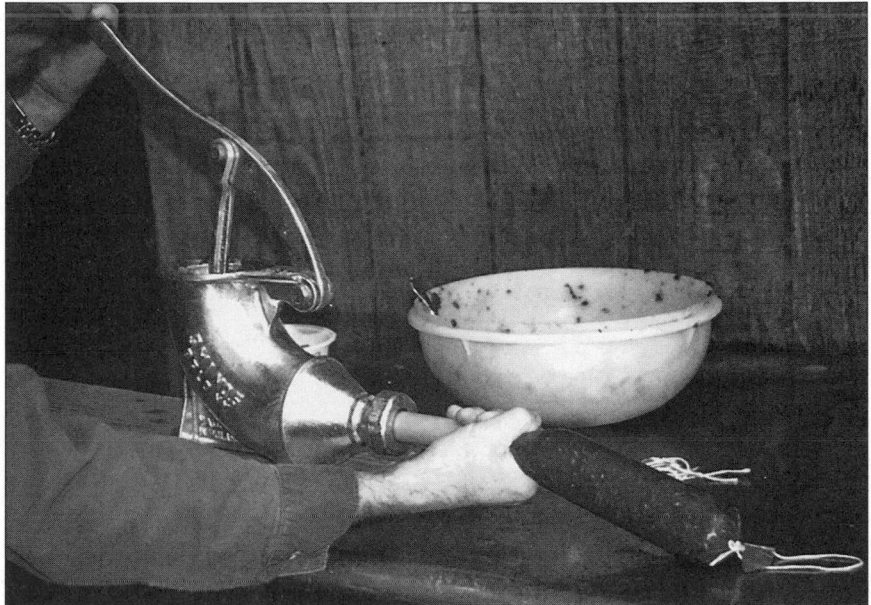

A larger volume of sausage can be stuffed using a stuffer such as this one from The Sausage Maker.

SMOKING SAUSAGES

If you have a commercial smoker that can reach 180 degrees F, you can smoke the sausages in it. Smoke at 140 degrees F for 1 hour. Raise the temperature to 160 degrees F and smoke for another hour. Then raise the temperature to 180 degrees F and smoke until the internal temperature of the meat reaches 160 degrees F. Use a meat thermometer inserted into the center of the sausage to test for the internal temperature. Test several sausages in different locations of the smokehouse to assure that the correct temperature has been reached.

Remove the sausages from the smoker, and shower them with hot water for a minute. Then spray them with cold water or place them in ice water to cool quickly. Sausages should be stored in a refrigerator at 40 degrees F or cooler. We like to vacuum pack the sausages and freeze them, taking out only one or two as needed. This way we have fresh sausages throughout the year for instant hors d'oeuvres anytime.

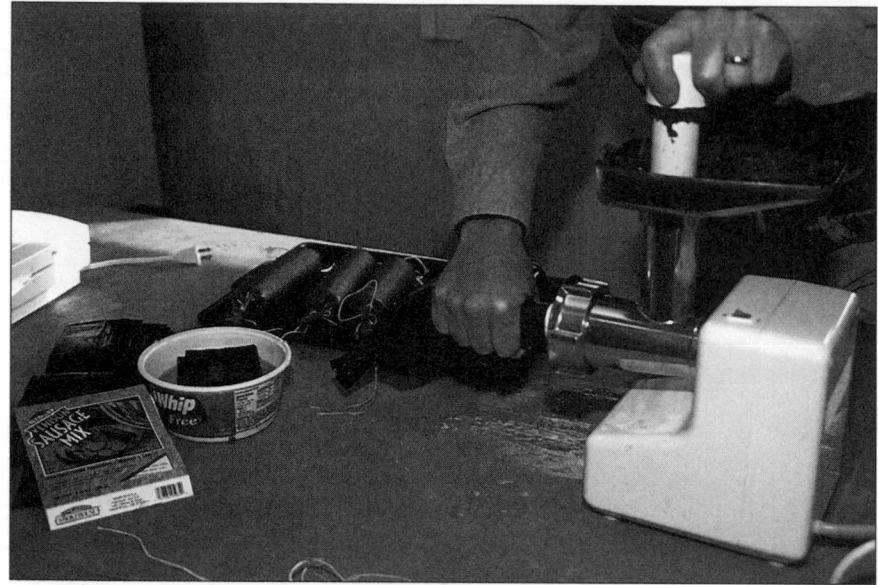

The quickest way to stuff casings is with a stuffing attachment on an electric grinder.

If using a cold smoker or homemade smoker that can't regulate or reach the temperatures needed, smoke at the hottest temperature available for a couple of hours. Then place the sausages in an oven set at 350 degrees F. The sausages can be placed on a cookie sheet. Bake until the internal temperature reaches 160 degrees.

CORNING VENISON

Venison can also be corned, or immersed in a brine as a preserving method. Corning definitely changes the taste of wild game and also acts as a tenderizer. You might want to try corning some venison the next time you're deciding what to do with the meat from that trophy buck.

The U.S.D.A. recommends the following recipe:

3 pounds (6¾ cup) salt
10 ounces (1⅜ cup) sugar
2½ ounces sodium nitrate
3 level teaspoons black pepper

3 level teaspoons ground cloves
6 bay leaves
12 level teaspoons mixed pickling spice

For onion flavor, add one medium sized onion, minced. For garlic flavor, add 4 garlic cloves, minced. Put the ingredients into a pickle crock or glass jar and add enough water to make a total of 6 gallons, including the ingredients.

The container should be covered. A good piece of round is wonderful corned, but less desirable cuts of meat like the brisket can be corned. The ideal temperature for corning meat is about 38 degrees F.

Place meat into the liquid. Put a heavy plate on meat; weight plate, if necessary, to keep meat below pickle brine.

Leave the meat in corning liquid for 15 days. On the fifth and tenth days, stir the liquid well, remove the meat, and put it back so the bottom piece is on top. Remove the meat after the fifteenth day. Use what you want immediately and store the balance in a cool place refrigerated at 38 degrees F. It is recommended that after meat is removed from the corning liquid it should be cooked and consumed within one week or frozen for up to one month.

The meat at this stage has a grayish pink color. When cooked, corned meat changes to the characteristic pink color associated with a cured product. Cook the corned meat as you would a corned beef brisket from the market. Simmer in water until tender.

EASY CORNED VENISON

Morton Salt has a simpler corned meat recipe. Mix Morton Tender Quick at the rate of two pounds Tender Quick per gallon of water needed to cover the meat. The water should have been boiled and cooled before using. Stir to dissolve the Tender Quick in the water and then pour over the meat packed in a clean crock or glass container. Spices may be added if desired. Morton suggests corning uniform pieces of meat so the curing time will be the same. The meat should stay in the cure about 2 days per pound with smaller pieces ready to use in about a week. Again, weight down the meat in the cure and refrigerate at temperatures between 36 and 40 degrees F while curing. After 5 days, take the meat from the brine, stir the brine and place the meat back in the brine with the top meat now on the bottom.

CORNED VENISON ROAST

A quick corned venison recipe that you can prepare any time of the year with a fresh boneless venison roast or even one from the freezer is simple to brine in the refrigerator.

2- to 3-pound venison boneless roast
2½ tablespoons Morton Tender Quick or Morton Sugar Cure
1 tablespoon brown sugar
1½ teaspoons black pepper
½ teaspoon paprika
½ teaspoon ground bay leaves
½ teaspoon allspice
¼ teaspoon garlic powder

Blend the spices into the Tender Quick or Sugar Cure. Rub this mixture into all sides of the roast. Place the meat in a plastic food bag and tie securely or place meat in a tightly sealed plastic food container. Refrigerate and allow to cure 5 days per inch of meat thickness. At the end of the curing time, cover with water and simmer until tender.

PRESSURE CANNING VENISON

Another method of preserving venison is by pressure canning the meat. Although canning is more time consuming than quickly freezing your game, canned meats require no electric power while stored and you don't have to wait for meat to thaw before preparing a meal. It also saves space if the meat is deboned and sliced or diced before canning. The meat can be precooked before canning or it can be packed raw. Whichever method you choose, process only quality chilled meat with all fat and connective tissue removed. Soak venison for an hour or so in a brine of 1 tablespoon salt for each quart of water needed to cover the meat. Rinse the brine from the meat before proceeding.

The sausages are then smoked to add flavor and to cure.

HOT-PACKED VENISON

Precook the meat. Pack the chunks or cubes of meat into canning jars, adding 1 teaspoon salt per quart. Fill the jars leaving 1-inch of headspace. Add boiling broth, water, or tomato juice to the jars, leaving 1-inch of headspace.

Ground venison can also be pressure canned. Brown the meat and pack into jars. Add boiling bouillon, water, or tomato juice. Add salt, adjusting the amount if adding bouillon. Again, leave 1-inch headspace. The ground venison can be loose packed, made into patties, or shaped into balls. Ground venison can only be hot packed.

RAW-PACKED VENISON

Fill jars with raw meat chunks or cubes, again leaving 1-inch of headspace. Add 1 teaspoon salt per quart jar. Do not add any liquid.

PROCESSING VENISON

Follow all recommended steps for pressure canning meats as given in the recipe book that came with your pressure canner. If your pressure canner is an older model, check with your local county extension office to see if the time and pressure recommended in your booklet are the current standards. Follow the current standard time and pressure recommendations for beef.

If you haven't previously canned any of your wild game, you should try at least a portion of this year's venison. Not only does the finished product have a different taste, but added convenience as well. The canned meat is ready to use in any of the recipes calling for boned, diced meat and most of the ground venison recipes.

FREEZING VENISON

One of the most common methods of preserving meat these days is by freezing. While simple and effective, there are limits to freezing's ability to maintain quality. Freezing protects from spoilage immediately but affects quality and flavor by drying out the meat. This is especially true in "frost-free" freezers, where moisture is pulled from the refrigerated air to prevent frost buildup.

It is important to handle meat correctly before wrapping. Remove all fat from the venison, because fat can often turn rancid, even while frozen. Freeze boneless meat such as the loin intact, rather than sliced ready to fry. Moisture escapes from each cut surface, speeding deterioration. Cut the meat as desired after it has partially thawed but is still firm enough to slice easily.

Wrapping Venison

Wrap the meat carefully to maintain quality for as long as possible. Heavy-duty freezer paper or aluminum foil can be used. Both are equally effective, although foil is easier to use on odd-shaped pieces. Plastic zippered freezer bags are a very convenient way of freezing portions of venison. A better method, however, is to double wrap, first using plastic food wrap, followed by freezer paper, aluminum foil, or a zippered bag. If using freezer paper, use freezer tape to seal the package together.

Above all else, mark the packages as to the contents and the month and year. You might also want to denote the specific trip, such as Kansas deer and trip date. Regardless of how careful we are about labeling, it seems that once or twice a year we pull out a mystery package with no label. What I thought was deer turns out to be dove. It all eats, but sometimes this causes a problem when you are planning a specific dinner for guests.

When wrapping meat, squeeze as much air from the package as possible.

Storage Times

You should plan to use all game within a year of freezing. Not only does this provide the best meat, but it is often necessary to follow some game laws regarding possession. Depending on how the meat is wrapped and what type of freezer is used, quality may remain constant for longer periods. Freezing for longer periods affects taste and quality but poses no other risks. The following chart gives an approximate storage guide for various cuts of meat.

Meat type	*Maximum storage*
Deer burger	4 months
Deer roasts	10 months
Deer steaks	8 months
Deer ribs	5 months

As you can see, the larger cuts of venison keep the longest. Rather than slicing into steaks, freeze a whole "steak section" and slice it after the meat has been thawed.

VACUUM PACKING

The ultimate method of preserving by freezing is using a vacuum-packing machine to remove oxygen from the container. Oxidation (exposure to oxygen in the air) is the main cause of food spoilage. When foods absorb oxygen, they begin a process of irreversible chemical change. Contact with oxygen causes foods to lose nutritional value, texture, flavor, and overall quality.

When oxygen is removed from the storage environment, foods can be stored three to five times longer than with conventional storage methods. In the absence of oxygen, dried foods, frozen foods, and perishable foods requiring refrigeration will retain their "just-bought" freshness and flavor much longer—resulting in less food waste.

Venison can also be canned, ready to heat and add to soup and stews.

Oxygen enables microorganisms such as bacteria, mold, and yeast to grow. These microorganisms cause rapid deterioration of food. Exposure to freezing cold air also causes "freezer burn" in frozen foods. (Freezer burn is localized dehydration.) Oxygen causes foods that are moderately high in fats and oils to yield a rancid odor and flavor. Air carries moisture, and moisture causes the food to become soggy and lose its texture. Moisture causes "caking" in dry solids, making them difficult to handle. Oxygen also allows insects to survive and hatch.

Preventing air from coming in contact with stored food is a two-step process:

Step 1. Remove all the air currently in the container.
Step 2. Prevent air from reentering the container.

This requires that two conditions be met:

1. The container needs to be made of a material which provides a barrier to oxygen.
2. The seal on the container needs to be air tight.

Vacuum packaging is the process of removing the air from a container so that a vacuum is created, and then sealing the container so that air cannot reenter.

Vacuum-packaging systems are able to create a vacuum in storage bags, canisters, jars, cans, and bottles. Storage bags used for freezing are especially designed to provide an oxygen and moisture barrier and to maintain an airtight seal. To provide an effective barrier, the bags should be constructed of plastic or a nylon layer. The bags should have a pattern of small "air channels" to ensure that air pockets don't form as the air is being removed.

It's important to choose the proper vacuum-packaging system. Bag sealers, sometimes thought of as vacuum-packaging systems, use a heated wire that welds the bag closed. They do not have any mechanism for removing air from the bag before sealing it. Bag sealers using a fan have a small rotary fan to extract some of the air out of the plastic bags before they are sealed. Some systems use polyethylene bags. Others provide sheets of plastic from which bags of different lengths can be made by "welding" the seams with a heated-wire bag-sealing mechanism. The fans in these models don't have enough suction to create a vacuum. The amount of air removed is comparable to using a straw to suck air out of the bag.

The plastic will shape itself loosely to the contours of the food in the bag, but it will be obvious that air remains in the bag. The type of bag material and the strength of the seal will determine whether oxygen is able to reenter the bag.

Electric-powered vacuum-packaging systems, such as the Food-Saver Professional II, eliminate exposure to oxygen. These systems extract the existing air in a variety of containers, including bags. The FoodSaver Professional II stores game in patented bags that keep food fresh three to five times longer and eliminate freezer burn.

Once a small package is vacuum packed, it stays fresh in the freezer for as long as 2 years—large cuts of meat stay fresh in the freezer for as long as 3 years. Plus, vacuum-packaged meat takes up less space in the freezer because it doesn't have to be packed in water.

Space the packages out in the freezer until they freeze completely. They can then be restacked to save space. Do not refreeze thawed raw meat. Thaw the meat in a refrigerator instead of at room temperature.

Meat to be frozen should be kept refrigerated at 40 degrees F or slightly cooler before freezing. Ground meats should be frozen within 2 days, whole cuts of venison within 3 to 5 days.

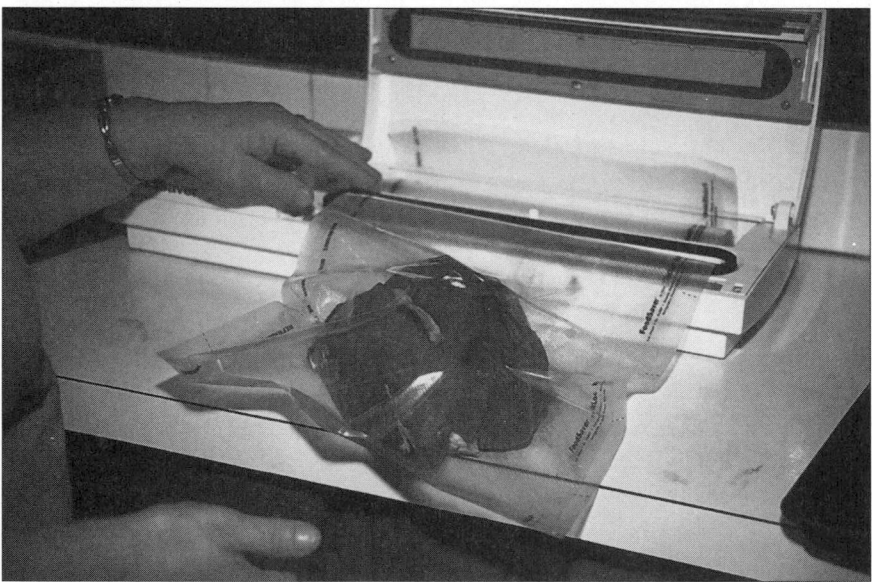

Freezing is one of the most common methods of preserving venison. The use of a vacuum packing machine greatly extends the life of the meat in the freezer.

CHAPTER 7

Cooking Tips and Safety

A wide variety of cooking methods can be used with venison. The method chosen depends on several factors. Venison can be fried, broiled, baked, cold smoked, hot smoked, corned, and made into jerky and sausages. One major consideration in the cooking method used is the age of the animal. Older deer, especially those old trophy bucks, tend to be tough. After sending the trophy antlers to the taxidermist, some hunters despair of turning the remainder of the big trophy deer into first-rate table fare. But if you keep the following tips in mind, any whitetail can enrich your menu.

OLDER OR TROPHY DEER

Meat can be marinated before cooking, but sometimes the easiest way to avoid tough, rubbery meat from older or trophy deer is to grind it up into burger or sausage. Grinding twice—once with a medium screen and once with a fine screen—is the most effective method. Some recipes specify 75 percent of the meat to be ground with a medium screen and 25 percent with a fine screen.

You can also get some of the benefits of grinding with judicious cutting. When sliced across the grain into thin steaks, the loin and backstrap of even big, old deer can still produce dishes that require binding arbitration to divvy up. Even roasts from old deer can be cooked to reasonable tenderness if they are sliced across the grain in half-inch slabs before cooking.

Slow and easy does it also helps. Any cut of meat will be more tender if cooked slowly. The difference in the tenderness of a roast cooked at 275 degrees F rather than 350 degrees F is well worth the extra time needed.

Corning is also an excellent way of tenderizing an older, trophy deer. The spices added to the corning brine will also eliminate the strong taste of many older animals.

Venison contains slightly more cholesterol than beef, pork, or chicken, but it has far less fat. This makes venison a heart-smart dietary choice. It also means that cooked venison can be dry—usually the most common complaint. But don't despair. The cure is easy.

Before Americans became cholesterol conscious, they "larded" dry meats by putting fat on or in a cut of meat before cooking. Basting with bacon grease or putting chunks of salt pork inside a roast still works great if you don't have to watch your fat consumption, and with this tactic you can use dry cooking methods like roasting or frying.

For those who want to limit dietary fat, the key to juicy venison is moist cooking. Putting a roast in a crock pot filled with water and vegetables is an option for large cuts. Steaks, chops, and cutlets can be cooked on top of the stove in a covered frying pan, again with plenty of liquid in the form of wine, tomato or cream sauces, or a combination.

The ultimate moist cooking method is stewing. Parts of a deer carcass that normally would be too tough for any other use can be cut into 1-inch chunks and used as the main ingredient for a hearty soup or stew. The natural enzymes found in fresh vegetables, aided by a few teaspoons of monosodium glutamate (MSG), work wonders during several hours of simmering.

Marinades can also do double duty. Soaking meat in various liquid concoctions before cooking can tenderize veteran venison while also reducing its gamey flavor.

For a 3- to 7-pound chuck, round, or rump roast, try this recipe from the Missouri Conservation Department:

6 bay leaves
12 whole cloves
1 tablespoon whole peppercorns
1 large onion, diced
Cooking sherry or white vinegar

Place the venison in a bowl, cover with equal parts dry wine or vinegar and water. Add the other ingredients. Place a plate over the meat to keep it down in the liquid. Refrigerate for 1 to 3 days, turning the meat several times.

Remove the meat from the marinade and sear on all sides in hot fat. Place on a wire rack in a covered roasting pan or baking bag and add a cup of marinade. Cook in a slow oven until tender, about 3 hours. Make gravy from the drippings.

YOUNG ANIMALS

Young deer provide succulent, juicy table fare. But they must also be cooked properly. Even the meat from younger deer tends to be drier than many other types of meat. It's easy to overcook or cook the moisture completely out of young venison. Some cuts even from young deer are tougher and harder to cook than others. It's best to cook the different cuts according to their inherent toughness. The loin and tenderloin areas make excellent steaks and chops, the hindquarters can produce steaks and round steaks. The ribs can be cooked as short ribs, although there's little meat on deer ribs, especially young ones. The remainder of the deer does best ground or cut into chunks for stew or soups.

Often cooks who are unfamiliar with wild game are puzzled. Forget the mystery or difficulty. Venison is extremely good table fare if (1) it is properly handled in the field, and (2) it is properly cooked. For the person in the kitchen, the first condition may be beyond his or her control. When the meat comes to the kitchen or camp stove, it's too late to fix things that have been abused by the hunter immediately after killing. Look at the meat, smell it, and if all seems well, go ahead with the cooking. The "wild" taste some people find objectionable can often be traced to improper handling in the field.

The first condition—proper field care and butchering—have been covered in previous chapters. The second condition—proper cooking—is the focus of this chapter. Two cardinal rules of cooking venison are very important. First, don't let it dry out. Second, don't overcook it. And these two rules are often linked.

Venison is extremely lean meat, and it doesn't fry well if you use conventional methods. Ground venison meat doesn't make into patties for fried or grilled hamburgers unless you add beef suet or some other ingredients to help hold the meat together. Yes, some deer meat cooks will dispute this point, but we're talking generalities here. If you want deer patties without the added fat, try broiling instead of frying or grilling or try some of the recipes in Chapter 9. Ground beef or pork can also be added to ground venison. If I want to serve grilled hamburgers, I mix pound for pound ground venison with the less expensive ground beef just before grilling. This method will add more than enough beef suet, yet the addition of the lean ground venison will keep your grilled burgers from shrinking.

Use venison almost any way you would use beef, with these precautions in mind: You can roast venison using moist heat methods and cook it to the medium or medium rare stage to an internal temperature of at least 160 degrees F. Usually venison doesn't make thick steaks along the line of a good, thick beef steak. Thin steaks, yes. These can be browned then simmered with something like mushroom soup until tender.

If you are new at cooking venison, try something like stew, spaghetti, or chili. Chances of success on the first attempt will be high if you have experience with these dishes. For stew, most people prefer cubed meat to ground meat. Cut the venison into half-inch cubes or the size you prefer, brown it quickly, then go ahead with your normal stew process. Potatoes, carrots, onions, tomatoes, and whatever spices you like won't make any change from your beef stew preparation.

Many persons who have worked with venison lean toward getting much of the deer carcass ground. This makes good use of the odds and ends of the deer meat after the hams, tenderloins, and other choice pieces are cut out.

Take a pound of ground venison, brown it slowly, then add it to your simmering spaghetti or chili. You won't be skimming off fat unless you've added a good bit of fat in the browning. Ground venison is great for spaghetti, chili, and other one-dish meals because you don't have to drain fat after browning and your kitchen isn't completely covered in grease splatter.

These two avenues—spaghetti and chili—are easy ones for the novice venison cook to travel. Ground venison, a jar of prepared spaghetti sauce like Ragu, and you're heading home free for a good meal you can brag about or wait for compliments. Ground venison, a package of chili mix from the grocery, and you're well on your way to a meal that will bring smiles from the successful deer hunters who have poked feet under your dining table.

SAFETY CONCERNS

Although wild venison is one of the safer meats, a few safety concerns must be addressed.

LYME DISEASE

Deer can be infected by ticks carrying Lyme Disease, and you can contract the disease. You are more apt to contract the disease while field dressing and skinning than through eating the meat. It is possible, although rare, however, to contract *Borrelia burgdorferi* in undercooked venison. In a recent study by researchers at the University of Wisconsin's Department of Food Sciences, it was found that *Borrelia burgdorferi* can survive in deer meat that is seared or cooked only to the rare stage. The bacteria is killed when the internal temperature of the meat reaches 160 degrees F for 2½ to 3 minutes.

In the past, meat to be used for jerky was first frozen, but there is no proof these days that freezing kills the Lyme Disease bacteria. It is best to expose the meat to a minimum temperature of 180 degrees F in a liquid marinade before the drying process. Venison summer sausage and other sausages that have not been cooked to a minimum of 160 degrees F internal temperature should be heated in a microwave oven before serving.

E. coli bacteria leaking or smeared from the intestines during field dressing can also contaminate venison, especially ground venison. *E. coli* can also be a problem if deer are not field dressed, skinned, or butchered immediately in hot weather or are left to hang in temperatures higher than 40 degrees F for any length of time.

For that reason, venison should be cooked to at least medium well done, or until the internal temperature reaches 160 degrees F. Jerky, which is often cured in a dehydrator, should be cooked until internal temperature reaches 160 degrees F in a liquid marinade. Bloody diarrhea and cramps are the common symptoms of *E. coli*.

CHRONIC WASTING DISEASE

Media reports recently linking eating wild deer meat to a form of "mad cow disease" have been sensationalized.

"The degenerative brain disease called chronic wasting disease (CWD) in deer and elk has occurred in Colorado and Wyoming for 30 years, but nobody who has hunted there or eaten venison from those animals has come down with CWD," said Mike Shaw, wildlife research supervisor for the Oklahoma Wildlife Department. "A hunter from Vinita, Oklahoma, contracted Creuztfelt-Jacob Disease, a related spongiform encephalopathy in 1999, but the National Center for Disease Control never established a positive connection to his eating deer meat. We even investigated the possible link by sampling sixteen deer from the area where the man hunted. None of the deer tested positive for chronic wasting disease. In addition, we have tested more than two hundred deer from other parts of the state, and those deer have all been negative for CWD."

A case of chronic wasting disease has been confirmed in a wild mule deer in southwestern Nebraska, although some captive elk have tested positive for the disease.

"Nationally, there are over 11 million big game hunters and only two confirmed reports of hunters contracting Creuztfelt-Jacob Disease," Shaw said. The center for Disease Control investigated both cases and concluded that their contracting CJD was coincidental to hunting.

"There is always a risk involved with handling any type of animals, domestic or wild, but that risk is very small," Shaw said. "The odds are many times greater that someone would be struck by lightning or die from a bee sting.

"As a biological scientist who has studied deer most of my life, I can honestly say that I don't see any danger in eating deer meat because there isn't any scientific evidence proving chronic wasting disease can cause Creuztfelt-Jacob Disease."

Shaw said there are two precautions that anyone concerned about chronic wasting disease can take. "Wearing protective gloves when dressing and butchering animals and avoiding consumption of brain and spinal cord tissue are good precautionary measures."

I would also suggest that you stay informed of any possible venison-related diseases in your state or the states or areas you hunt.

One of the major reasons for doing your own butchering is wild game meat to be ground is usually mixed together from different animals at the processing plant. Other less careful hunters may allow contamination of their meat by feces and other means. By processing the meat yourself you can control what you and your family eat.

CHAPTER 8

Smoke Cooking and Barbecuing

S moke cooking—with indirect heat—or hot smoking (barbecuing), with direct heat are both excellent methods for cooking venison. Smoke cooking is a southern tradition. Parked behind many a barn or shed in my part of the Ozarks is a homemade smoker. Today, however, a variety of manufactured cookers and smokers make smoking and smoke cooking easy and reliable.

Three types of "smoke" cookers are available. The first type is the simple barbecue grill, either charcoal or gas. You either pile on the charcoal briquettes or light the gas and cook with the heat. Charcoal adds some smoke flavor, and wood chips can be added to the ignited charcoal as well as to most gas grills for added smoke flavoring.

The second type of smoke cooker is a moist-heat smoker. It has a high dome with a lid and a separate pan to hold a marinade. Moistened wood chips are added for smoking. A number of these smoke cookers are available, including models from Cabela's, Brinkman, Coleman, and Bass Pro Shops. Both of these smoker/cookers cook by direct heat.

True smokers, however, use indirect heat. They are quite often larger models of welded metal to maintain more consistent heat, and are capable of handling much more fire as well as more meat at one loading. Smokers cook by indirect heat, with the coals in one area of the smoker and the meat in another. A number of these smokers are available, but the best I've tested is the Good-One Grill and Smoker from Ron Goodwin Enterprises. The Good-One is available in several sizes, from small to large commercial models. All are built with the same basic design. The front lower compart-

Cold-smoke cooking is an excellent method of cooking venison roasts.

ment is the firebox and grill. You can grill just as you would with any charcoal grill. The upper back compartment, however, is for smoking or cooking meats with lower, indirect heat. On the lower front of the firebox are the air control dampers to control the heat in the firebox and grill area. On the top of the smoker lid is an exhaust vent. The heat in the smoker is controlled by the dampers. The smokers are constructed with a clean-out pan located under the firebox grate.

To smoke, the top grate is removed from the bottom compartment and charcoal placed on the bottom grate. You'll need about 10 pounds of charcoal for several hours of smoking. After coals are burning, add the wood chunks to provide the smoke flavor and close the bottom lid. Just as in any smoking, the type of wood chunks used provide the flavoring. These types of smokers do not use water pans. "Water pans make steam heat, which can cause smoke to disappear rapidly and tends to make meat soggy," said Ron Goodwin. "We don't recommend water pans for true, old-fashioned pit barbecue flavor." Ron also suggests using pure charcoal chunks rather than briquettes, although the former are a little harder to obtain. "Another secret to good barbecue smoked meat is a smoker that will hold an even temperature and the right amount and kind of wood," Ron added. "Hickory, mesquite, oak, pecan, alder, or fruitswoods (cherry, peach, apple or grapevine) are recommended. Poultry requires much less wood than other meats, and gamebirds and waterfowl are very good if smoked using fruitwoods. The best result for smoke flavor is to use chunks of wood, two or three chunks: about 3 to 4 inches in size usually give a nice smoked flavor."

Maintaining an even temperature over a long period of time is important for ease in smoke cooking. The Good-One Grill and Smoker has a temperature gauge and a variety of means of regulating the heat. By simply opening and closing the dampers, you can control the heat precisely. You will also need a meat thermometer to check the internal temperature of the meat.

Smoke cooking is an excellent method for cooking a venison roast or ham (hindquarter) because it keeps the moisture in the meat rather than drying it out. Even the relatively dry meat of venison comes out moist and for the most part tender.

For a venison roast, ham, or hindquarter, cook the meat at 275 to 300 degrees F for 2 hours, then cut the smoker temperature back with the damper to 225 degrees F. Finish cooking at that temperature for 1 hour for each pound of meat. Use a meat thermometer, and cook until the internal temperature reaches 180 to 190 degrees F. Wrapping venison in bacon strips will add some flavoring and also keep the meat from drying out.

I've also discovered that regardless of the meat being smoked, I prefer to smoke for about an hour or two, then wrap the meat in foil for the remainder of the cooking process. This tends to hold in even more moisture. The roast or ham can be basted with barbecue sauce, left natural, or basted in a number of sauces.

GAME BARBECUE SAUCE

Following is a game barbecue sauce recipe from Dave Korsi:

1 32-ounce bottle catsup
4 tablespoons vinegar
¼ cup Worcestershire sauce
2 to 3 tablespoons Liquid Smoke, to taste
3 to 4 tablespoons orange liquor (TripleSec)
½ to 1 teaspoon garlic powder

1 tablespoon chili powder
1 to 3 teaspoons dried minced onion
⅓ cup brown sugar, firmly packed
4 tablespoons molasses
¼ teaspoon ground dry mustard
¼ teaspoon ground cayenne pepper

Mix all ingredients in saucepan and simmer 20 to 30 minutes, stirring occasionally. Let cool before serving. Keeps 3 to 4 weeks in the refrigerator.

SWEET AND SPICY BARBECUE SAUCE

1 32-ounce bottle catsup
1 12-ounce bottle chili sauce
½ cup bottled steak sauce
¼ cup Worcestershire sauce
1 12-ounce can beer
⅓ cup prepared mustard
1 tablespoon dry mustard
1½ cups lemon juice, vinegar, wine vinegar, or wine
1½ cups firmly packed brown sugar
2 tablespoons black pepper
1 teaspoon garlic powder

Mix all ingredients. Pour into containers. Will keep in the refrigerator for 3 to 4 weeks or can be frozen for later use.

DRY RUBS

Many chefs prefer to use a dry rub on meats to be barbecued, and this works quite well with the smoking process and venison for the initial smoking. I then prefer to add the liquid sauce for the latter portion of the smoking process. Following are a couple of basic rub recipes that can be adjusted to suit with more or less of the peppers to adjust the heat. Spices your family doesn't like can be left out and any you like can be added. One rub has a basis of paprika with very little salt added and the other has a salt base. Brown or white sugar can also be added for a sweet version.

Paprika-Based Dry Rub

½ cup paprika
1 tablespoon chili powder
1 tablespoon ground black pepper
1 tablespoon lemon pepper
1 tablespoon ground cayenne pepper
1 tablespoon crushed red pepper flakes
1 teaspoon garlic salt
1 teaspoon garlic powder
1 teaspoon onion salt
1 teaspoon onion powder
1 teaspoon celery salt
1 teaspoon dry mustard

Mix all together and store in an airtight container. Rub on the outside of chops, steaks, or roasts before smoking or grilling.

Salt-Based Dry Rub

1 cup salt
1 cup ground black pepper
1 cup paprika
1 cup sugar
2 teaspoons garlic powder
2 teaspoons onion powder
3 teaspoons chili powder
2 teaspoons dry mustard
½ teaspoon cayenne pepper
1 teaspoon ground thyme
1 teaspoon ground oregano

Mix all together and store in an airtight container. Rub on the outside of chops, steaks, or roasts before smoking or grilling.

Grilling Venison

Venison steaks and chops can also be grilled directly on the barbecue grill. Since venison is a very dry meat, it's best to marinate or baste the meat in an oil-based marinade before grilling. Our favorite

Venison steaks and chops are also excellent grilled.

is simply basting the meat in garlic butter. Grill over hot coals 5 minutes to a side or until done to suit.

Following are a few other favorites:

GRILLED SOUTHWEST BACKSTRAPS

1 pound venison backstrap, butterfly cut to ½ inch thick
1 1.25-ounce package southwest marinade

Prepare the marinade according to the directions on the package. Marinate in the refrigerator at least 30 minutes. Grill 5 minutes to a side over hot coals, then move away from the coals to finish smoke cooking. Grill plenty of backstraps because anything leftover will make great fajitas.

VENISON KABOBS

Venison steak or loin, cut into 1-inch cubes
Sweet red pepper, cut into 1½ inch dice

Mushroom caps, 1 to 1½ inches in diameter
Large, sweet onion (Vidalia or Texas sweet), cut into wedges
Zucchini, 1 inch diameter, cut into 1 inch chunks
Italian salad dressing
1 teaspoon dried crushed red pepper flakes

Marinate the venison cubes in Italian dressing with the red pepper flakes stirred in. Marinate at least 1 hour or overnight. Prepare the vegetables and sprinkle Italian dressing over them. Alternate the meat cubes and vegetables on skewers. Skewer the zucchini chunks side to side through the skin rather than through the center. Grill over hot coals, turning often and basting with Italian dressing. Serve with foil-baked potatoes from the grill.

TERIYAKI VENISON KABOBS

Venison steak or loin, cut into 1-inch cubes
Sweet red pepper, cut into 1½ inch dice
Mushroom caps, 1 to 1½ inches in diameter
Large, sweet onion (Vidalia or Texas sweet), cut into
    wedges
Pineapple chunks, drained, liquid reserved

Teriyaki marinade
1 package teriyaki sauce, prepared as directed using reserved
    pineapple juice for the liquid.

Marinate the venison in a teriyaki marinade at least 1 hour or overnight. Prepare the vegetables. Drain the pineapple chunks and prepare the envelope of teriyaki sauce. Pour the remainder of the pineapple juice over the vegetables and pineapple chunks and toss to coat. Prepare skewers, alternating meat, vegetables and pineapple chunks. Brush often with teriyaki sauce while grilling. Serve over rice with additional teriyaki sauce.

GRILLED VENISON FAJITAS

Venison steak
Marinade, southwest or mesquite
Sweet red or green pepper, cut into strips

Sweet onion, cut into lengthwise strips
Flour tortillas

Marinate the venison steak in your favorite south-of-the-border marinade. We like the flavor of Southwest Marinade which is hot and spicy, but mesquite is a less hot choice. Marinate at least 1 hour, but overnight is great. Grill the steak over hot coals 5 minutes to a side then move away from the coals to cook to desired doneness. When the steak is almost done, toss the vegetables with a little marinade, Italian salad dressing, or olive oil. Grill in a basket until roasted. Meanwhile wrap a stack of flour tortillas in aluminum foil and warm on the grill away from direct heat. Slice the steak into thin strips and let your guests prepare their own fajitas.

Grilled Venison Burgers

2 pounds ground venison
1 cup bread crumbs
2 eggs, beaten
2 tablespoons catsup, steak sauce, or Worcestershire sauce
½ teaspoon garlic powder
1 teaspoon salt
½ teaspoon pepper
Sliced bacon

Place the ground venison in a large bowl and sprinkle the garlic powder, salt, and pepper over the meat. Add the bread crumbs and beaten eggs. Add the catsup, steak sauce or Worcestershire sauce 1 tablespoon at a time and mix until all the crumbs are absorbed. Shape into patties and wrap one slice of bacon around the edge of each burger. Grill over hot coals, turning carefully.

CHAPTER 9

Recipes

I've been hunting deer with gun and bow for more than four decades, not only on my own property and home state, but often in other states during my writing career. I've also been a long-time muzzleloader deer hunter, and the result is usually a fair amount of venison. In addition, all of my kids, my wife Joan, a nephew, and numerous friends are part of our deer-hunting camp. We've tried just about every recipe you can imagine for venison. Most of it is good, some just better than others. Almost any recipe you like to use for beef can be used for venison—sometimes with slight adjustments.

We've included the many venison recipes my wife and I have tested as well as a number of recipes from friends, hunting buddies, and some hunting lodges and camps I've had the pleasure to visit over the years.

QUICK SKILLET BURGERS

1 pound ground venison
1 package dry onion soup mix
1 tablespoon oil
1 cup water

Mix the ground venison with 1 tablespoon of the dry soup mix. Shape into four patties. Pour the oil in a heavy skillet and use a brush to coat the bottom and sides of the skillet with oil. Brown the meat patties on both sides. Stir the remainder of the soup mix in the water and pour over the burgers. Cover and cook over low heat for about 15 minutes. Uncover and cook until the liquid glazes the patties. Serve on buns or as a main dish.

Venison Loaf

2 pounds ground venison
1 package dry onion soup mix
½ to 1 teaspoon black pepper
1 to 2 teaspoons Italian seasoning
1 teaspoon garlic powder
4 slices white or light wheat bread torn into pieces
1 cup tomato juice
1 cup quick oats
4 eggs, beaten
Catsup

Place the ground venison in a large bowl. Sprinkle the dry onion soup mix, pepper, Italian seasoning, and garlic powder over the ground meat and mix in. Pour the tomato juice over the bread pieces and mix in the blender or food processor until smooth. Mix the oats, eggs, and tomato-bread mixture into the ground meat. Add oats or juice if the mixture is too dry or too soft. Form into a loaf and place in a greased loaf pan or 9 × 13 baking dish. Spread the catsup over the top of the loaf and bake at 350 degrees F for 1½ hours or until done.

Mexican Loaf

Follow the directions for Venison Loaf, replacing the tomato juice with taco sauce in mild, medium, or hot to suit taste. Instead of the Italian seasoning, add 1 teaspoon cumin. Garnish the top with catsup mixed with hot sauce. Bake as above.

Pizza Loaf

Follow the directions for Venison Loaf, replacing the tomato juice with pizza sauce. Garnish the top with catsup and sprinkle on additional Italian seasoning. Bake as above. Place triangles of mozzarella cheese on top of the loaf and return to the oven a few minutes until melted. Serve with a salad and garlic bread.

Pizza Casserole

½ recipe Pizza Loaf (above)
1 jar pizza sauce
1 cup shredded mozzarella cheese
1 16-ounce package curly noodles

Prepare a half-recipe of Pizza Loaf and shape into four patties. Place in a greased casserole and bake at 350 degrees F for 30 minutes. Cook the noodles according to package directions. Drain the noodles immediately, stir in the pizza sauce, and about half the cheese. Spread the noodles over the baked patties and sprinkle the rest of the cheese on top. Return to the oven for 15 to 20 minutes.

Note: This recipe can also be made with leftover baked Pizza Loaf. Simply slice any leftover Pizza Loaf and place in the bottom of a greased casserole. Add the noodles prepared as above and heat in the oven until warm.

Quick Skillet Stroganoff

1 pound ground venison
Oil
1 package dry onion soup mix
1 can cream of mushroom soup
1 small can sliced mushrooms, drained
1 8-ounce carton regular or light dairy sour cream
1 16-ounce package noodles

Brown the ground venison over low heat in 1 tablespoon oil. Stir and break up the meat as it browns. When the meat is well broken up and browned, stir in the dry soup mix. Mix the mushroom soup with one soup can water and whip with a wire whisk or blend until smooth. Pour over the meat and add the mushrooms. Cook the noodles in boiling salted water and let the Stroganoff simmer while the noodles are cooking. When the noodles are done, stir the sour cream into the Stroganoff and serve the sauce over the noodles. Serve with a salad and garlic bread.

SPAGHETTI SAUCE

2 pounds ground venison
Oil
Salt and pepper
1 large onion, diced
1 large green pepper, diced
2 teaspoons Italian seasoning
2 cloves garlic, minced or pressed
2 whole bay leaves
2 14.5-ounce cans diced tomatoes (can be with green chilies,
    roasted garlic, or favorite)
1 6-ounce can tomato paste
1 4-ounce can mushroom slices

Brown the ground venison in a heavy bottomed 6-quart saucepan. Brown slowly over a low heat using as little oil as possible. Add salt and pepper, onions, green pepper, Italian seasoning, garlic, and bay leaves. Cook until the vegetables are tender and the meat is brown. Stir often to break up the venison. Drain the canned tomatoes into a bowl and whip the juice into the tomato paste. Stir the tomatoes and paste into the sauce. Add drained mushroom slices. Simmer over a low heat to desired thickness. Adjust seasonings to taste and remove the bay leaves before serving. Serve over spaghetti or use in Lasagna or Spaghetti Casserole.

SPAGHETTI CASSEROLE

1 package thin spaghetti
1 recipe spaghetti sauce
Mozzarella cheese, shredded

Cook the spaghetti, following package directions, then drain and spread in a glass or stainless-steel 9 × 13 baking dish. Spread the sauce over the spaghetti and spread the cheese on top. Bake until warm and cheese has melted.

Note: We usually make this recipe of leftover spaghetti and sauce and freeze to have a quick meal on busy days. Save some of the cheese to add after the casserole is heated through.

LASAGNA

1 recipe spaghetti sauce
1 16-ounce package lasagna noodles
1 24-ounce carton small curd cottage cheese
3 eggs
1 to 1½ cups grated Parmesan cheese
Mozzarella cheese, grated

Cook the lasagna noodles in a large pan to keep from breaking up the noodles. Drain and rinse in cold water. Beat the eggs with a wire whisk until lemon colored. Stir in the cottage cheese and Parmesan cheese. The mixture should be fairly stiff, not runny. Place enough spaghetti sauce in the bottom of a glass or stainless steel baking dish to just cover the bottom. Place a layer of lasagna noodles over the sauce. Spread a layer of the cottage cheese mixture, then sauce, mozzarella cheese, noodles, cottage cheese mixture and so on until the dish is full.

Note: This will make two casseroles unless you have a really large lasagna dish. We often bake a 10 × 14 dish for guests and freeze a small casserole dish for later.

VENISON CUTLETS PARMIGIANA

Venison steak or tenderloin
4 slices fresh, white bread
¼ cup Parmesan cheese
1 egg, beaten
¼ cup milk
Salt and pepper
Oil
Spaghetti sauce
Sliced mozzarella cheese
Fettuccine noodles

Remove all sinew from the venison and pound between sheets of waxed paper with the flat side of a meat mallet until ¼ inch thick. Process the 4 slices of fresh bread in a food processor to fine crumbs. Mix the crumbs with ¼ cup Parmesan cheese. Beat the egg with the ¼ cup milk. Dip the cutlets into the egg/milk mixture. Pour a portion of the crumbs onto a flat plate and place the cutlet from the milk mixture onto the crumbs. Salt and pepper the cutlet and turn over to coat the opposite side. Dip each cutlet, adding more crumbs to the plate as needed. Fry the cutlets in oil over medium heat for approximately 5 minutes per side. Remove the cutlets from the skillet and keep warm. Drain any remaining oil from the skillet, pour a half-inch layer of spaghetti sauce in the skillet, and heat. Return the cutlets to the skillet, place a slice of cheese on each cutlet and heat until the cheese warms. Serve over fettuccini noodles.

These cutlets can be served in a number of ways. We often prepare a double batch of cutlets, serving the fresh batch with pan gravy and mashed potatoes, then freeze the remainder with waxed paper between each cutlet. To serve the fettuccini version, simply heat the spaghetti sauce in a skillet, add the frozen cutlets, and heat. Add the sliced cheese and serve. The meal is ready in the time it takes to cook the fettuccini.

Enchilada Casserole

1 pound ground venison
Oil
1 jalapeno pepper or 1 sweet green pepper,
    diced
1 medium onion, diced
Cheddar and Monterrey Jack cheese, shredded
1 can enchilada sauce or 1 package enchilada sauce prepared
    according to package directions
12 corn or flour tortillas

Brown the ground venison in as little oil as possible. Add the pepper and onion and brown. Stir in a little enchilada sauce just to moisten. Lightly grease or spray a 9 × 13 glass baking dish. Place some of the meat mixture down the center of each tortilla and roll. Place seam side down in the baking dish. Pour the enchilada sauce around and over the tortilla rolls and spread cheese over the top. Bake until warm and the cheese is melted. Serve with shredded lettuce, diced tomatoes, and refried beans.

STUFFED PEPPERS

4 green peppers
1 pound ground venison
1 small onion diced
1¼ cups instant rice
1 can whole kernel corn
1 14.5-ounce can diced tomatoes with roasted garlic
Salt and pepper
1 teaspoon Italian seasoning
½ cup tomato juice
Grated cheese

Brown the ground venison and the onion over a low heat, breaking up the meat as it cooks. Stir the rice, corn, and tomatoes into the meat and onions. Salt and pepper to taste, and add seasonings. Cover and cook on low until rice is tender. Remove seeds and wash the green peppers. Stuff each pepper with the meat mixture and stand in a baking dish. Pour the tomato juice around the peppers. Garnish the top of each stuffed pepper with a little grated cheese. Bake in a 350-degree F oven until the peppers are tender.

SKILLET GOULASH

1 pound ground venison
Salt and pepper
Oil
1 onion, diced
1 14.5-ounce can diced tomatoes with green chilies
1 14.5-ounce can diced tomatoes with roasted garlic
1 8-ounce can tomato sauce
4 cups water
2 7.25-ounce boxes macaroni and cheese dinner

Brush oil on the inside of a large, heavy saucepan. Brown the venison and onion in the saucepan. Salt and pepper the meat. Add the water along with 1 teaspoon salt. Bring the water to a boil and stir in the macaroni from both boxes. Return to a boil, stirring to mix. Turn the heat to low and cover the pan. Cook 10 minutes or until the macaroni is tender and liquid is absorbed. When the liquid is absorbed, stir in the tomatoes and tomato sauce. When the macaroni is tender stir in the cheese packages and heat through. Serve with a tossed salad and garlic bread.

Pizza Burgers

1 pound ground venison
1 small onion, diced
1 small green pepper, diced
1 can sliced mushrooms, drained
½ cup sliced black olives
1 14- or 15-ounce jar or can of pizza sauce
Mozzarella cheese
Hamburger buns, loaf of Italian bread, or purchased pizza crust

Brown the venison, onion, and pepper. Stir in the pizza sauce and mushrooms, and simmer until thick and warm. Stir in the black olives just before serving. Serve on buns with slices of cheese. Or slice the loaf of Italian bread lengthwise through the center. Place the two halves cut side up on a cookie sheet. Spoon the meat mixture onto the bread and top with overlapping triangles of cheese. Heat in a 350-degree F oven for 5 to 10 minutes or until cheese melts. Cut each into 2 to 4 pieces and serve as pizza. Or spread the meat mixture on a pizza crust, top with shredded mozzarella cheese, and bake until crust is warm and cheese is melted.

Crowd Pleasing Chili

4 pounds ground venison
3 onions, diced
3 green peppers, diced
4 tablespoons chili powder
2 tablespoons ground cumin
Salt and pepper
3 14.5-ounce cans diced tomatoes with green chilies
3 cans tomato sauce
1 111-ounce can chili beans in mild or hot sauce

This recipe requires a large, heavy-bottomed soup or stew pot. Brown the ground venison in the bottom of the pot. Brown slowly, stirring often to break up the meat. Add the onions and green peppers and cook until the onions are transparent and peppers are tender. Salt and pepper the meat, then add the chili powder and cumin. Add the tomatoes and simmer 30 to 45 minutes. Add the chili beans and tomato sauce. Simmer at least another 30 to 45 minutes and adjust seasonings to taste. This large recipe will serve a crowd or can be frozen.

Note: If you prefer a really mild chili, plain diced tomatoes can be used.

REAL VENISON CHILI

1 12- to 16-ounce package hickory smoked bacon, diced
3 pounds venison cut into ½ inch chunks or coarse ground
1 large or 2 small onions, chopped
1 12-ounce can beer
1 large can vegetable (V-8) juice
1 4-ounce can chopped green chilies
1 can tomato paste
4 to 6 tablespoons chili powder
1 to 3 tablespoons ground cumin
3 cloves garlic, minced
Salt and black pepper

Brown the diced bacon in a large pan. Remove the bacon and drain. Brown the venison in the bacon grease. Add the onion and cook until transparent. Return the bacon to the pan and add the remainder of the ingredients. Simmer over low heat, tightly covered for at least 2 hours. Adjust seasonings. Add beans of your choice or serve over beans.

STOVE-TOP VENISON STROGANOFF

1 pound venison tenderloin, cut into thin strips or bite-size pieces
Flour
Oil
Salt and pepper
1 package dry onion soup mix
1 can sliced mushrooms
1 can cream of mushroom soup
1 8-ounce carton sour cream

Salt, pepper, and flour the venison and brown in oil. Remove from the skillet and drain the meat pieces on layers of paper towels as they brown. When all the meat is browned, pour off excess oil and stir flour into the pan scrapings. Add the dry onion soup mix and 2 cups water. Return the meat pieces to the skillet and simmer until the meat is tender. (**Note:** If using less tender cuts of venison, this may need to simmer for an hour or more.) Add more water if needed. When the meat is tender, add the mushrooms and stir in the mushroom soup. Simmer until the mixture is smooth and thick then stir in the sour cream just before serving. Serve over noodles.

BAKED STEAK

Venison steak
Salt and pepper
Flour
Oil

Salt and pepper the steak and pound in the flour. Brown the steak in oil in a heavy, cast-iron skillet with a tight lid. As the steak is browned, remove to drain on paper towels. Scrape the pan drippings and stir in flour. Add water and stir until the gravy is smooth. Return the steak to the skillet, pushing each piece down into the gravy. Cover the skillet and bake in a 325-degree F oven until the steak is tender and the gravy thick. Serve with mashed potatoes.

Note: For variety, dry onion soup mix or cream of mushroom soup may be added to the gravy.

SWISS STEAK

1 venison round steak, 1-inch thick
Oil
Flour
Salt and pepper
1 large onion, diced
1 large or 2 small green peppers, cut in a large dice
2 small (1 to 1½ inch diameter) zucchini, (one yellow, one green) sliced
2 14.5-ounce cans diced tomatoes with roasted garlic
2 teaspoons Italian seasoning

Trim the round steak and cut into serving pieces. Salt, pepper, and flour each piece and tenderize. Add more flour as needed. Brown the steak pieces in oil in a large cast-iron skillet with a tight lid. When the meat is brown, remove from the skillet and pour off excess oil. Scrape the pan drippings and stir in a little flour, then ½ cup water. Put the steak pieces back in the skillet (preferably in one layer) and place the onion, peppers, and zucchini over the steak. Pour the tomatoes and juice over all. Sprinkle on the Italian seasoning and salt and pepper the vegetables. Cover and bake at 325 degrees F until the steak is tender. Add more water if needed. Bake potatoes or a potato casserole in the oven at the same time.

SPYDER'S VENISON PIE

This recipe is from my deer hunting friends at Buck Hollow Ranch in Arkansas. This individual meat pie recipe is the Americanization of pies served in the Limpopo Valley of South Africa. Spyder Stanley, chief cook at the Tschipise Camp, Greater Kuduland Safaris shared the following with us in autumn of 1996.

1½ pounds roasted venison shoulder, shredded (approximately a
    1-quart freezer bag of shredded meat)
1 large onion, chopped
1 4-ounce can mushrooms, pieces & stems, undrained
3 tablespoons margarine
2 tablespoons soy sauce
2 tablespoons currant jelly
3 tablespoons parsley flakes
2 tablespoons Worcestershire sauce
2 teaspoons garlic powder
2 teaspoons ginger
¼ teaspoon nutmeg
2 1.1-ounce packages Hunter Sauce Mix (Knorr or McCormack)
3 boxes Pillsbury 9-inch pie crusts
1 egg, beaten

Bake venison shoulder in oven at 325 degrees F for 3 hours, let cool, then shred into ½-inch pieces by hand or with a knife. Set aside 1½ pounds with some of the meat drippings. Freeze the excess for another recipe.

Sauté chopped onion in margarine until opaque, add mushrooms with liquid, venison, and all the spices. Heat through, drain the meat mixture, saving the liquid.

Cut pie crusts in half, fill with drained meat mixture, crimp edges with a fork, and prick crust for venting. Brush beaten egg lightly over pies. Bake on lightly greased cookie sheets at 350 degrees F about 15 minutes or until light golden brown.

Follow directions on the Hunter Sauce Mix and add to the meat mixture liquid. Bring to a boil and simmer. Serve individual pies with sauce to the side.

VENISON ROAST AND GRAVY

1 venison chuck roast, 2 inches thick
Flour
Salt and pepper
Oil
1 teaspoon Kitchen Bouquet

Brush the inside of a cast-iron Dutch oven with oil. Salt and pepper one side of the roast and flour. Place the roast in the Dutch oven, flour side down, and brown. While one side is browning, salt and pepper the other side and flour. Turn to brown the other side. When both sides of the roast are brown, add water to not quite cover the roast and add a bit more salt and the Kitchen Bouquet to the water. Cover tightly and place in a 325-degree F oven. Bake until tender or at least 2 hours. Remove from the oven and carefully remove the roast to a heated platter. Stir or shake flour and water to remove lumps then stir into the pan drippings and cook until gravy thickens.

DEER ROAST

This recipe comes from the Secret Cook Book of Louisiana's Hackberry Rod and Gun Club.

Medium deer roast
3 tablespoons olive oil
1 can cream of mushroom soup
1 can onion soup
Salt and pepper
Flour

Garlic powder
3 tablespoons Worcestershire sauce

Brush the inside of a medium-size roaster with olive oil. Sprinkle salt, pepper, and garlic powder on the roast. Lightly flour the roast. Place the roast in the roaster unbrowned. Heat the soups and Worcestershire sauce until blended and pour over the roast. Bake, covered, at 350 degrees F for 3 to 4 hours or until tender.

ONE-POT MEAL

1 small venison chuck roast, 2-inches thick
Flour
Salt and pepper
Oil
2 onions, quartered or several pearl onions
4 to 6 carrots, scraped and cut into 1-inch pieces
4 to 6 potatoes, peeled and cut in half or quartered
½ head cabbage, cut into wedges

Salt, pepper, and flour the roast and brown in oil in a large cast-iron Dutch oven. When brown on both sides, add water to almost cover the roast. Place the onions, carrots, and potatoes around the roast and salt and pepper the vegetables. Lay the wedges of cabbage on top and salt and pepper the cabbage. Cover tightly and cook in a 325-degree F oven until the meat and vegetables are tender. This one-pot meal will also cook on top of a wood heating stove. Serve this in large, flat bowls because the broth is delicious.

EASY VENISON STEW

1½ pounds venison cut in 1-inch cubes
Oil
Salt and pepper
Flour
1 envelope brown gravy mix
2 1-pound packages frozen stew vegetables

Salt and pepper the venison cubes and roll in flour. Brown in oil a few pieces at a time. As the meat browns, place it in a slow cooker. Stir flour into the pan drippings, add the gravy mix and 2 cups water. Cook and stir until well blended, then pour over the meat in the slow cooker. Stir in the thawed stew vegetables and salt and pepper to taste. Cook on low for 6 to 8 hours.

DEER CAMP STEW

4 heaping cups cubed venison
Salt and pepper
Flour
Oil
2 cups chopped onion
4 beef bouillon cubes
4 cups water

Salt and pepper the venison chunks and roll in flour. Brown a few at a time in oil in a large cast-iron Dutch oven. Remove from the pan as they brown and drain on paper towels. When the meat is all browned and draining, brown the onion. Stir 4 tablespoons dipping flour into the pan. Stir until flour is absorbed. Dissolve the bouillon cubes in 4 cups water and stir into the pan drippings. Add the browned meat, cover tightly and simmer until the venison cubes are tender.

4 cups peeled, diced potatoes
3 cups scrapped, diced carrots
1 1-pound bag frozen peas
1 1-pound bag frozen whole kernel corn

While the venison chunks are simmering, prepare the potatoes and carrots and cook in separate pans in salted water until tender. When the venison chunks and vegetables are tender, drain the potatoes and carrots and stir into the meat chunks. Add the peas and corn. Simmer at least another one-half hour. Serve with slices of fresh baked bread.

CAMP LIVER AND ONIONS

One of the favorite foods in deer camp is fresh liver. It's easy to prepare in a Dutch oven over a campfire and a great way to celebrate the hunt. Wash the liver thoroughly and allow to drain. Remove the bile sack and connective tissues, then slice into ¼-inch pieces.

Fresh deer liver, sliced
Flour
Oil
2 to 3 large sweet onions, sliced
Salt and pepper
2 or 3 beef bouillon cubes
Water

Pat dry the liver slices on paper towels, then salt, pepper, and flour. Brown in ¼-inch oil in a large Dutch oven. Remove the liver slices as they brown and drain on paper towels. Brown the sliced onion. Stir two or three tablespoons of the flour into the pan drippings and stir until flour is absorbed. Dissolve the bouillon cubes in a cup of water and stir into the drippings. Return the liver slices to the pan, pushing them down into the onion slices. Add water to cover and additional salt and pepper. Cover the Dutch oven and cook until the liver is tender and the gravy thick. Serve with mashed potatoes.

Sweet Pepper Soup

1 pound ground venison
Salt and pepper
4 cups beef broth or beef bouillon dissolved in water
1 large onion, diced
2 green peppers, diced
1 cup instant rice
1 15-ounce can whole kernel corn
2 14.5-ounce cans diced tomatoes
Few dashes hot pepper sauce
Shredded cheese

Brown the ground venison slowly, stirring and breaking up the meat as it browns. Add the onion and cook until transparent. Stir in the green peppers and beef broth. Add the remaining ingredients and simmer until all is tender and flavors blended. Adjust seasonings and add hot pepper sauce to taste. Garnish each serving with shredded cheese.

Taco Soup

1 pound ground venison
Salt and pepper

2 large onions, diced
1 green pepper, diced
1 sweet red pepper, diced
2 14.5-ounce cans diced tomatoes with green chilies
4 cups beef broth or beef bouillon dissolved in water
Shredded cheese

Salt and pepper the venison and brown. Add the onions, peppers, tomatoes, and broth. Simmer until all is tender and well blended. Adjust seasonings. Other hot peppers may be added to suit. Garnish each serving with shredded cheese and serve with corn chips.

VENISON MINCEMEAT

One deer neck
Salt
6 cups ground apples (3 pounds or approximately 12 medium apples, cored and coarse ground)
3½ pounds seedless raisins
1 quart applesauce
2 quarts apple juice
1 tablespoon ground cinnamon
1½ teaspoon ground cloves
1½ teaspoon ground ginger
¼ teaspoon ground nutmeg
¼ teaspoon ground allspice
1 pound brown sugar
½ cup white sugar
1 to 2 tablespoons flour

Simmer one deer neck covered in water until tender and meat starts falling from the bones. Add 4 to 6 teaspoons salt to the water. Remove meat from the broth and let meat cool so that all fat hardens. Discard cooking liquid. Remove meat from bones and discard all fat. Grind meat and measure 2 quarts ground meat.

In a large, heavy pan mix remaining ingredients except white sugar and flour and simmer stirring often until mixture is thick and raisins are plump. Taste, adding more spices if desired. Blend together sugar and flour and stir into mincemeat; simmer 10 more minutes. Mincemeat is ready for pies, the freezer, or it may also be pressure canned.

Nutrient content of lean[a] domestic and game meats.

Species	Moisture	Protein	Fat	Cholesterol	Energy[b]
	g/100g			mg/100g	Kcal/100g
Beef (USDA Choice)	70.2	22.0	6.5	72	180
Beef (USDA STD)	73.2	22.7	2.0	69	152
Pork	71.9	22.3	4.9	71	165
Lamb[c]	73.2	20.8	5.7	66	167
Buffalo	74.5	21.7	1.9	62	138
Whitetail Deer	73.5	23.6	1.4	116	149
Mule Deer	73.4	23.7	1.3	107	145
Elk	74.8	22.8	0.9	67	137
Moose	75.8	22.1	0.5	71	130
Antelope	73.9	22.5	0.9	112	144
Squirrel	73.8	21.4	3.2	83	149
Cottontail	74.5	21.6	2.4	77	144
Jackrabbit	73.8	21.9	2.4	131	153
Chicken	75.7	23.6	0.7	62	135
Turkey (domestic)	73.8	23.5	1.5	60	146
Wild Turkey	71.7	25.7	1.1	55	163
Pheasant (domestic)	74.0	23.9	0.8	71	144
Wild Pheasant	72.4	25.7	0.6	52	148
Grey Partridge	72.1	25.6	0.7	85	151
Sharptail Grouse	74.2	23.8	0.7	105	142
Sage Grouse	74.3	23.7	1.1	101	140
Dove	73.6	22.9	1.8	94	145
Sandhill Crane	73.2	21.7	2.4	123	153
Snow Goose	71.1	22.7	3.6	142	121
Mallard	73.2	23.1	2.0	140	152
Widgeon	73.5	22.6	2.1	131	153

[a]Mammal Samples—Longissimus Muscle
Avian Samples—Breast Muscle
[b]Determined by bomb calorimeter.
[c]Results of research conducted at North Dakota State University. All values (except lamb which is published in *The Journal of Food Science*) are the result of original research at North Dakota State University. Some of these results have been published.

Sources

API, Outland Sports, Inc., 417-451-4438, www.outlandsports.com
ATSKO, Sno-Seal, Inc., 803-531-1820, www.atsko.com
Alaska Game Bags, Inc., 907-522-3221, www.alaskagamebags.com
Allied Kenco Sales, 800-356-5189, www.alliedkenco.com
Bass Pro Shops, 800-BASS PRO, www.basspro.com
Bill Harper's Seasonings and cookbooks, 573-346-1779
Bowhunters Discount Warehouse, 800-735-BOWS,
    www.bowhunterswarehouse.com
Bradley Smoker, 800-665-4188, www.bradleysmoker.com
The Brinkmann Corp., 800-527-0717, www.thebrinkmanncorp.com
Buck Knives, 800-326-2925, www.buckknives.com
Cabela's, 800-237-4444, www.cabelas.com
Charlie's Horse, North Coast Outfitters, Ltd., 888-558-8108,
    www.charlieshorse.com
Chef'sChoice, EdgeCraft Corp., 800-342-3255, www.edgecraft.com
Excalibur Dehydrators, www.excaliburdehydrator.com
FoodSaver, Tilia, 800-777-5452, www.foodsaver.com
Game Locker, 888-246-4342, www.gamelockercoolers.com
Good-One Smokers, Ron Goodwin Enterprises, 620-726-5281,
    www.thegood-one.com
Hackberry Rod and Gun Club, 337-762-3391, www.hackberry-
    rodandgun.com
Hunter's Specialties, 800-728-0321, www.hunterspec.com
Katz Knives, 800-848-7084, www.katzknives.com
Kawasaki, 800-661-RIDE, www.kawasaki.com
Lawry's Foods, 800-9LAWRYS, www.lawrys.com
L.E.M. Products, Inc., 877-536-7763, www.lemproducts.com
Little Chief Smoker Products, Luhr-Jensen & Sons, Inc.,
    800-366-3811, www.luhrjensen.com

Masterbuilt Mfg., Inc., 800-489-1581, www.masterbuilt.com
Mister Tenderizer, 800-383-0990, www.mrtenderizer.com
Morton Salt, www.mortonsalt.com
Normark Corp., 800-874-4451, www.rapala.com
Original DeerLife, 800-738-LIFT
Pa-Paw's ATV Game Hoist, 888-4PA-PAW'S
Rack-A-Deer, Professional Hunting Products, LLC, 616-789-1507,
    www.prohuntproducts.com
ROBCO Mfg., 800-849-5511, www.robcomfg.com
Roleez Hunteez, 800-369-1390
Rule Industries, Inc., 978-281-0440
San Angelo All-Luminum Products, Inc., 800-531-7230
Strongbuilt DeerStands, 800-255-5536
The Sausage Maker, Inc., 888-490-8525, www.sausagemaker.com
Thunderbird Food Machinery, Inc., 800-7-MIXERS
Trax America, 800-232-2327
Uncle Mike's, Michaels of Oregon Co., 503-655-7964,
    www.michaels-oregon.com
Warn Industries, 800-543-WARN
Warren & Sweat Manufacturing Co., Inc., 352-669-3166, www.war-
    renandsweat.com
Weston Supply, 800-814-4895, www.westonsupply.com
Working Class Products, 877-PRO-CART

Proper Processing of Wild Game And Fish, Penn State College of
    Agricultural Sciences, Agricultural Research and Cooperative Ex-
    tension, compiled by Catherine N. Cutter, Assistant Professor, De-
    partment of Food Science, Penn State, 2000

Forget The Woods, MU Scientist Says Venison Should Be In
    the Meat Case, MU News, November 12, 1999, University of
    Missouri-Columbia.

Oklahoma Venison and Elk Safe to Eat, News Release, June 15,
    2000, Oklahoma Department of Wildlife Conservation.

USDA, www.fsis.usda.gov

Index